DATE DUE

FEB 0 4 2014	
March 03, 2015	

D1172475

Water from Stone

NUMBER FORTY-ONE
Louise Lindsey Merrick
Natural Environment Series

WATER FROM STONE

The Story of Selah, Bamberger Ranch Preserve

JEFFREY GREENE

ILLUSTRATIONS BY MARGARET BAMBERGER

TEXAS A&M UNIVERSITY PRESS   COLLEGE STATION

Library of Congress Cataloging-in-Publication Data

Greene, Jeffrey, 1952–

Water from stone : the story of Selah, Bamberger Ranch Preserve / Jeffrey Greene ;

illustrations by Margaret Bamberger.—1st ed.

p. cm.—(Louise Lindsey Merrick natural environment series ; no. 41)

Includes bibliographical references and index.

ISBN-13: 978-58544-593-6 (cloth : alk. paper)

ISBN-10: 1-58544-593-2 (cloth : alk. paper)

1. Natural history—Texas—Bamberger Ranch Preserve.

2. Bamberger Ranch Preserve (Tex.)   I. Title

QH105.T4G74   2007

508.764'64—dc22

2006030393

For Mary & Margaret

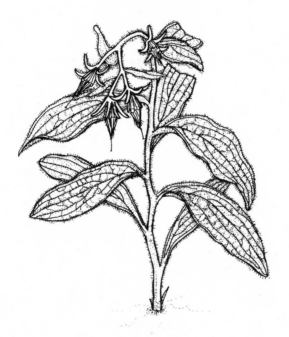

MARBLESEED *Onosmodium helleri*

I knew in my heart that we as a nation were already farther along the path of destruction than most people knew. What we needed was a new kind of pioneer, not the sort which cut down the forests and burned off the prairies and raped the land, but pioneers who created new forests and healed and restored the richness of the country God had given us, that richness which, from the moment that the first settler landed on the Atlantic coast, we had done our best to destroy. I had the foolish idea that I wanted to be one of that new race of pioneers.

–Louis Bromfield, *Pleasant Valley*

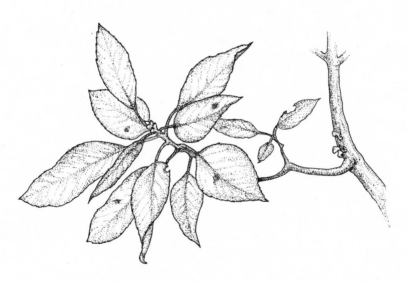

TEXAS MADRONE *Arbutus xalapensis*

GOLDEN-CHEEKED WARBLER *Dendroica chrysoparia*

Contents

PINK EVENING PRIMROSE *Oenothera speciosa*

Acknowledgments

The material in this book is in large part anecdotal, taken primarily from informal conversations with David and Margaret Bamberger. However, friends, family, and acquaintances of the Bambergers made essential contributions. I am grateful to Colleen and Scott Gardner, Tom Bamberger, Donna Belle Bamberger, Deena Ray Sessums, Margie Crisp, Jim Berry, Steven Fulton, Scott Grote, Jim Smith, Ralph and Terrie Kovel, Don and Donna Airhart, Louise Allen, and Wendy Smith.

I am particularly grateful to Shannon Davies, the Louise Lindsey Merrick Editor for the Natural Environment at Texas A&M University Press, who took an interest in this book from its very conception, educated me in Texas environmental issues, and saw this project through its various stages, including her work with Margaret on the illustrations. I want to thank Thom Lemmons, Managing Editor at Texas A&M University Press, for his numerous improvements to this text, and Mary Ann Jacob for her attractive book design.

I'm indebted to Leonilda and Peter Wainwright for generously providing me with a base in the United States and transportation for the two months when I covered thousands of miles. Finally, I'm indebted to Richard Farrell for his close reading of my work over the years. Deepest thanks to Susan Prospere and Charles Siebert.

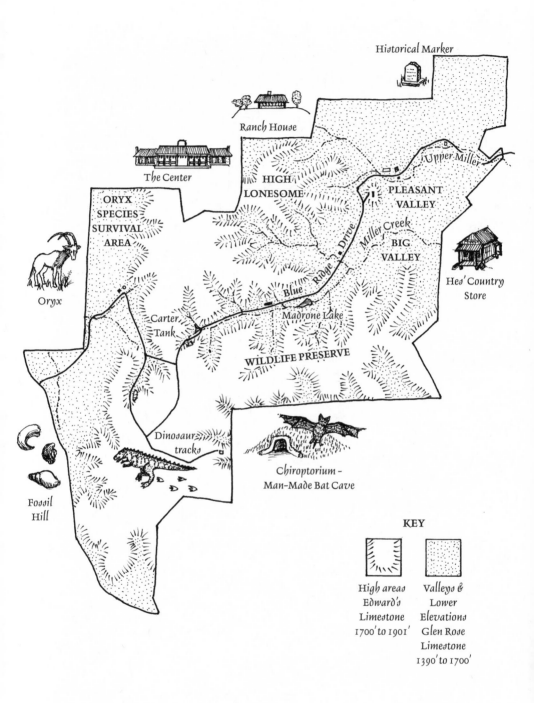

Historical Marker

Ranch House

The Center

ORYX
SPECIES
SURVIVAL
AREA

HIGH
LONESOME

Upper Miller

PLEASANT
VALLEY

Miller Creek

BIG
VALLEY

Oryx

Blue Ridge Drive

Carter
Tank

Madrone Lake

Hes' Country
Store

WILDLIFE PRESERVE

Dinosaur
tracks

Chiroptorium -
Man-Made Bat Cave

Fossil
Hill

KEY

High areas
Edward's
Limestone
1700' to 1901'

Valleys &
Lower
Elevations
Glen Rose
Limestone
1390' to 1700'

Water from Stone

TEXAS BLUEBONNET *Lupinus texensis*

The Grass Trail

THE FIRST DAYS of the new year at Selah began in freezing mist, wind-driven, so that the rock outcroppings, live oaks, and whitened ponds seemed to trawl through clouds and patches of blown rain. The deer appeared baffled by the half-light that wouldn't wake into day; a gray fox, usually nocturnal, rummaged behind dormitories at The Center. The raw weather made it appealing to be indoors, where the fire that my brother-in-law David Bamberger had made radiated from a fireplace large enough to warm a semicircle of comfortable chairs. But I had just driven from New York City via Biloxi, New Orleans, and Houston, all closed in by the same fog, a uniform dreaminess that blanketed swamps, skyscrapers, bridges, coastal washes, and the familiar limestone hills. The whole south of the nation had fallen under a spell. I needed to get out and walk.

The Selah ranch house is situated on a rise between the lower pastureland to the east called Windsong and a hill and upper pasture to the west called High Lonesome. To the northeast, where Miller Creek runs toward the Pedernales River, is Malabar and then, next to it, Pleasant Valley, names honoring Ohio's Louis Bromfield, the novelist and screenwriter who transformed himself into America's foremost activist for land restoration. Farther north is an airstrip erased in the distance, abruptly de-listed by the FAA when its last arrival, uninvited, had ended in pieces in the trees. I walked south past a makeshift shooting range, where hunters must prove facility with a rifle to avoid accidents and minimize the number of wounded animals staggering about. The road descends gently. A turn left leads to Jacob's Ladder Tank, but straight takes you past Hes' Country Store and on the rise to the right the Recycle

Cabin. I walked to the very heart of Selah, through the gate announcing the Wildlife Preserve and a convection of trails bearing the names of renowned naturalists.

Near Madrone Lake and the Nature Trail that runs up to The Center, there is a small garden on the right devoted to native grasses. It once displayed eighty-four species. The Grass Trail wound through the different grasses, and in the winter fog they seemed all the more dormant and skeletal. Yet when I looked closely, the individual plots of grasses—some as tall as I am, others rising barely an inch, the stems feathery, spindled, or spear-like—made small structural worlds of their own. Of the features of the Texas Hill Country, the grasses are among the most magnificent, so varied and yet unified as surroundings for the trees, rocks, creeks, ponds, canyons, and cattle.

When I recall my first visit, in January 2000, with my wife, Mary, one scene in particular comes to mind: the African grass area called "The Sahara" behind Little Mexico, where the Mexican laborers live on the ranch. It is the endangered species section devoted to the scimitar-horned oryx, no longer found in the wilds of its native North Africa. As elegant and powerful as these large animals appear, their horns arcing three feet over their backs, it was the way the grasses formed a savannah and the way the slope at the edge of the small plateau opened out over the far hills that I found so striking. This particular landscape provides a vague window on what the Hill Country might have looked like in the time of the buffalo and then the arrival of the first German and Irish settlers, except for the Kleingrass that had been planted specifically for the sheltered antelope. It was the grasses that fueled dreams of empires of cattle and sheep, never to be, engendering a cycle of mutual demise of landscape and rancher, the fragile soil unable to support the pressures of livestock or agriculture. Whole towns failed.

David, who restored the land and created a nature preserve, would say that the story of Selah is the story of water. While the Hill Country appeared to have water—thirty inches a year—it was susceptible to very high evaporation rates, and often the rain arrived in seasonal deluges, dissipating quickly, and eroding the soil as runoff once grass and root systems were disrupted. It was a delicate system: soil retaining water, grass retaining soil. Few things give David as much pleasure as showing people the land, explaining these fragile balances and offering the sense and means by which we can all contribute to their conservation.

I was at home in Paris when Mary quietly celebrated an unlikely Christmas and New Year's at Selah with her sister Margaret Bamberger and her family. That autumn, Margaret came close to death after failed chemotherapy and then hospitalization for lung and liver cancer, her daughter Margie providing day and night care. Mary spent most of October and part of November in Texas trying to keep up Margie's spirits and helping out as she could before finally leaving Texas when Margaret was stabilized, soon to return home for final hospice care. By New Year's, however, thanks to a last-ditch effort using a molecularly targeted drug, Margaret began a recovery so uncanny that it left both us and all the extensive network of her friends in a state of awe.

Sometimes there are feelings that run deeper than gratitude, and their power, as romantic transcendentalists will affirm, finds an inexplicable correspondence in the movement of autumn trees or in morning light catching the slope of mountains or in a silent freezing mist descending over grasses. A visceral appreciation of such correspondences is the only claim I can make to being a naturalist. I can't explain the chemistry of chlorophyll and the color green, I forget the names of wildflowers as fast as I learn them, and my hands are so unsteady with binoculars that there's no discernible difference for me between an earth tremor and the flicking of a black-capped vireo in shrubs or of a golden-cheeked warbler in juniper and hardwood. I am completely deprived of the pleasures of hunting, an experience with special bonds to father, brothers, family, and friends; the way heightened senses tune in to the patterns and signs of an animal's presence; our instinct for the kill; the ethic of it. And above all, Texas is not a native landscape for me, though I lived six years in Houston.

As I walked the Grass Trail, I knew that there was much to learn about native Texas grasses and the Selah story. I already knew that

David had to restore the grasses before water would return to former creek beds. The grasses would control runoff and erosion. Also, one could read the geological qualities of the land by where the grasses grew, where the seeps were and the clay. The grasses would provide an array of uses, including forage, wildlife cover, and birdseed. And what could be more delicate than the panicled inflorescence of plain lovegrass or bolder than the eastern gamma seedhead that Colleen Gardner, the ranch's assistant director, described to me as "a grassy version of the bird-of-paradise flower"? Margaret had assembled numerous pamphlets for Selah's nature education workshops, and I remember in particular her pen-and-ink drawings of grasses: bushy bluestem by the water and seep muhly by the damp ledges.

Over the years, it became clear to me that the story of Selah—the evolution of its programs and philosophies as well as its future prospects—is inextricably bound to my brother-in-law's own story, his unlikely trajectory from door-to-door vacuum cleaner salesman to co-founder and board chairman of Church's Fried Chicken to spokesman for environmental policy at local, federal, and international levels. His story is not inspirational because he attained considerable wealth through industry and imagination. He undoubtedly could have amassed a far greater fortune. It is, however, inspiring because an early passion for nature instilled in him by his mother and his rural Ohio beginnings combined with entrepreneurial instincts led to an entirely unique approach to selling environmental causes. Growing up in the Great Depression inured him to a reflexive sense of resource conservation, and his business success provided the boldness and means to experiment. While David's background and the making of Selah form the body of this book, it was the additional story of Margaret's recovery that suggested moving parallels for me. The book imposed itself urgently, and though it is a tribute to two worshippers of nature, its other subject is the nature of survival: how our individual survival and our habitat affects all of us.

All inspirational stories are in large part fiction, if for no other reason than their omissions in service to a narrative line. There are always

inconsistencies, struggles with human weaknesses, and a myriad of contributions by good-hearted people who go unrecognized. There is also
the fiction created when the experience of another is processed through a
writer's imagination. Inaccuracies, however unintentional, are inevitable.
As David often says, "Memory is the poorest record of history."

At first I had imagined pointed lessons from two naturalists, but
what occurred was more anecdotal: long conversations in Texas, spending days and evenings with Margaret and David, often joined by others,
sharing stories and knowledge. Experts would take me aside and explain
how some preposterous mode of behavior or unlikely morphology can
ensure the survival of an organism. I'm not a botanist or ecologist or
even an informed amateur naturalist. I'm no David, and even he says of
himself, "I don't speak genus and species." Still, learning is excitement,
and teaching is a mission at Selah. While noting the stories of David's
life and the making of Selah, a different sort of collaboration emerged:
Margaret gathering strength; talking to groups again; appearing at public
events, including the Relay for Life in the neighboring town of Blanco;
and finally walking—a few hundred feet at first, then up to a mile or so,
to render the features of Selah with penpoints and inks for this book
while I'm five thousand miles away, putting together these words.

The Historical Marker

JUST THREE MONTHS after my January visit, I returned, and David Bamberger and I waited to intercept a busload of USDA International Programs staff members arriving at the "tomb for mankind." The staff members from the Washington D.C. area were attending a conference in Austin, and the Texas Forest Service treated them to a tour of the Bamberger Ranch Preserve, known as Selah, only fifty miles directly west, near Johnson City, boyhood home of Lyndon Baines Johnson. I'd like to say it was hot for April, but what I quickly learned about the Texas Hill Country is that temperatures can fluctuate by forty degrees not only from day to day but also from one hour to the next, so extremes feel normal.

April is one of the Hill Country's months of splendor. Highways, ranch roads, trails, loops, and farm-to-market roads are bordered with firewheels, greenthread, wine cup, prickly poppy, skull cap, and Texas stars, let alone the celebrated bluebonnets and paintbrush that the highway department has programmatically distributed since the 1930s. Lady Bird Johnson encouraged this proliferation by promoting an initiative to halt roadside mowing until wildflowers had had sufficient time to seed themselves. Recently, two Texas magazines both ran, unbeknownst to each other, spring wildflower features, and on one Sunday a 22,000-car procession invaded small Hill Country roads, creating city-like traffic jams and requiring the scrambling intervention of the sheriff's department. The wildflower tourists, mostly from Austin and San Antonio but even from Dallas and Houston, stopped to photograph the stunning displays, spread out picnics, and use any available stand of trees as a restroom. People discarded trash randomly; no one had anticipated a need for roadside receptacles. The wildflower sightseeing phenomenon was clear evidence of the potential for nature tourism, but ranch owners, for whom privacy is sacred, were enraged. They posted stern promises to prosecute trespassers and vengefully mowed down the wildflowers on or even near their property. Some raised hell at the county commissioner's office. Others put their property up for sale.

David and I walked in the heat to Miller Creek, where in limpid water we saw a largemouth bass almost absurdly oversized for the pool formed by one of Selah's concrete dams, each with a low-water crossing. The large bass was in fruitless pursuit of a smaller, quicker one. I couldn't decide if the behavior was cannibalistic, territorial, or both. I've seen red-eared sliders and yellow mud turtles in the creek, along with green herons, kingfishers, and an occasional languid water snake. City visitors, including me, automatically assume that any water snake is nothing less than a deadly cottonmouth since snake stories abound in Texas, usually involving cottonmouths dropping out of trees and into fishing boats or showing up like nightmares on the ends of fishing lines.

It was almost impossible to imagine that this creek, with running water year-round, was mostly dry just a few decades ago. The USDA staff soon learned that the restored natural spring is at the very heart of the Selah conservation story and that producing and controlling water is rapidly becoming one of the most important issues in Texas, as in other states—and countries, for that matter. One need only take a map of Texas and trace a triangle, I-35 between San Antonio and Dallas/Fort Worth with Austin along the way, then I-45 to Houston, and I-10 back to San Antonio, to see the explosive growth and population pressure on an area that for the most part could hardly support the pioneers only a hundred and fifty years ago. Now with the prospect of privatization, Texas faces the possibility of having to purchase water, an essential natural resource, much like oil.

At the time, however, David's concern was simply to cut off the bus early enough to have it park away from the marker, which would serve as his introductory podium for the tour. All too often, he has hollered over the rumbling of engines that drivers usually leave idling. As soon as the USDA bus had passed the panels for grazing management and land stewardship awards and pulled up ten minutes late, four freshly air-conditioned Texas Forest Service agents in crisply pressed uniforms descended, lifting their sunglasses and shaking David's hand, then mine after David introduced me as his brother-in-law from Paris, France.

The bus driver not only followed David's directive to park away from the marker but also kindly killed the engine while the group of fifty USDA staff, remarkably diverse in age and ethnic background, assembled before the "tomb for mankind." Despite the marker's ominous message, the group was in soaring spirits; after all, it was a stunning April day, the Texas hills at the pinnacle of wildflower season, the birds flashy in their courtship rituals and domestic planning. I overheard a tall, middle-aged African American forester, continuing a conversation begun on the bus about cloning, say, "I would pay $5,000 to see a wooly mammoth. Wouldn't you? You know what a wooly mammoth is, don't you?"

We are already becoming attuned to more exotic forms of nature tourism on the order of *Jurassic Park* and civilian flights into space; however, the mention of wooly mammoths was more appropriate to Selah since we were gathering in front of a stone erected as a warning of humanity's potential extinction. Wooly mammoths have been extinct for only 10,000 years and were depicted with a dreamy sophistication in red ochre cave paintings by upper Paleolithic people who were the first master artists of France and Spain. David erected the monument for humankind approximately fifteen feet from the road, and the stone itself stands no taller than two feet high. A low stone wall with iron grillwork surrounds it. The marker reads:

IN MEMORY
OF MAN
2,000,000 B.C.–A.D. 20 ?
HE WHO ONCE
DOMINATED THE EARTH

— 9 —

DESTROYED IT
WITH HIS WASTES,
HIS POISONS AND
HIS OWN NUMBERS

In a sense, the historical marker is a necessity. If the extinction of human-kind is to be mourned, we obviously have to do it, in advance, ourselves. Who else will?

David, 5'10" with pure white hair, a few strands of which often fall across his forehead, stood on the low stone wall, gripped the iron grill, and disposed himself to his audience with a lively country accent, peculiarly Texan, despite his having grown up in Ohio. "I'm going to start talking up here, and I get so wound up your whole two hours might go right by. I'm David Bamberger, like hamburger, but you put your 'B' on it. You can't forget it that way." Of course, people know that it was chicken—David having co-founded and board-chaired the Church's Fried Chicken fast-food chain—and not hamburgers that facilitated his purchase of the forsaken land that would become the Bamberger Ranch Preserve. "I was a salesman, and people would remember me because they'd say, 'He said it was something like hamburger.' Their remembering helped me make a little money."

David couldn't resist the irony. After all, before making his fortune in the fried chicken business and subsequent enterprises, he had spent seventeen years during the 1950s and 1960s trying to support a family and gain a comfortable life through one of the toughest and least respected of businesses: door-to-door vacuum cleaner sales in Ohio, Oklahoma, and Texas. I imagined the mnemonic working another way: a guy with a lousy job comes home to learn that some son of a bitch named "Hamburger" has sold his wife a damn vacuum cleaner behind his back.

Bamberger continued, "I want to tell you a short story before we get moving. I was born in Ohio, and I'm now seventy-seven years old. We didn't have electricity or running water in the home until I was four, so our mom sent us down the hill to a neighbor who had a well with a hand pump. We had to carry the water in a milk bucket. When a four- or five-year-old kid carries an open bucket full of water, by the time he gets home, he's lost half of it on his leg. Someone said, 'That's why you became a conservationist. You're careful with water.' I said, 'Well, that's right.'"

The audience from D.C., many of whom undoubtedly grew up in some of our bleakest neighborhoods, was anything but naïve. They'd been steeped in the myth of the "American self-made man," in this case the folksy appeal of an impoverished childhood set to rights, in later life, by the owning of an impressive piece of now-valuable Hill Country landscape. The big twist, also not lost on this audience of foresters, was that Bamberger, who could be enjoying all the trappings of wealth—travel, expensive cars, and country clubs—intended not only to give away to future generations everything he built, in the form of a nature preserve, but also to devote whatever remained of his years, and his determined heart, to environmental education and saving endangered species. What he asked for in return was simply a platform from which he could speak for the protection of the natural world. He invariably used his own biography to personalize his proselytizing, environmental activism.

At that moment, the platform happened to be a phony historical marker with a stark warning reminiscent of the grim fable Rachel Carson used to introduce her book *Silent Spring*, on the damage caused by DDT: "No witchcraft, no enemy action had silenced the rebirth of new life in this stricken world. The people had done it themselves." Likewise, Bill McKibben, with the same candor but less artifice, sounded the alarm on global warming. "I believe without recognizing it we have already stepped over the threshold of such change: that we are at the end of nature." It was a telling paradox that on a stunning day in a paradisiacal setting, everyone was forced to contemplate our contributions to the end of the world. The environmental policy message from the very administration under which the USDA operated was "learn to adapt," rather than take steps to change our ways.

David told the story behind his erecting "the tomb for mankind." The controversial Endangered Species Act had just been passed, and the ranch and its programs were receiving attention from the Sierra Club, Texas Forest Service, Texas Parks and Wildlife Department, and many other conservation organizations. David said, "People think I'm kinda crazy, but I believe that I'm related to these leaves here on the trees and these grasses and these bees and insects. The relationship can't be explained yet; maybe it will never be totally explained. It's mysterious. But if you destroy a species, you destroy part of us. When you 'dust' enough species, you 'dust' mankind."

The gravestone had been on a neighbor's place, and he'd had no idea of what to do with it besides give it away. David gladly took it, eager to have it engraved as a warning at the entrance to Selah. He brought it to a stonecutter in San Antonio, who understandably assumed that David had just had a death in the family and was respectfully quiet while David introduced himself and talked some. The stonecutter took off his hat, looked at the marker, and asked, "Who will we be honoring on the stone?" David handed him a piece of paper with the text he wanted. The engraver's demeanor changed radically. He said, "Well, I'll be damned. I've made tombstones for cats and dogs and canaries and horses. This is the first time I've buried the whole human race."

One evening, David and I drank "Jim Rhoades," a highball concocted of Seagram's and 7-Up that David named after Selah's long-term arborist, who had introduced him to it. David routinely requested "Jim Rhoades" in bars and restaurants, sending the bartender hopelessly to his cocktail reference books. It was definitely not a drink that would appeal to everyone. It sent Margaret's nose into wrinkles of aversion, although, in the absence of a light beer, she'd partake. Because I'd come in from Paris but much prefer American to French steak, David grilled sirloins from the hybrid beef-buffalo stock he called Grassmasters. Much of what I learned about Selah took place on spring evenings with Margaret and David on the ranch house terrace, eating more steak and drinking more Jim Rhoades than advisable, while the Bambergers' exuberant dog

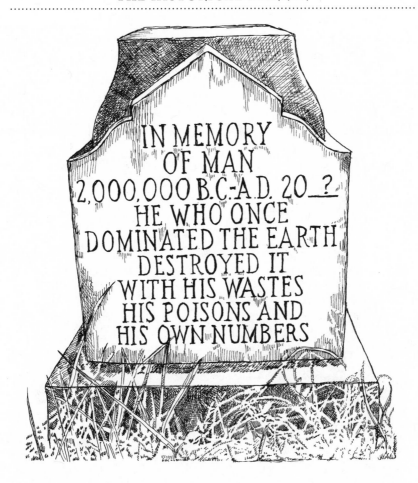

IN MEMORY
OF MAN
2,000,000 B.C.–A.D. 20__?
HE WHO ONCE
DOMINATED THE EARTH
DESTROYED IT
WITH HIS WASTES
HIS POISONS AND
HIS OWN NUMBERS

Corey wildly chased my two Maltese dogs across the lawn like startled rabbits. Small, elegantly coiffured, and pure white, Pandora and Snowbell were the last animals anyone would expect on a Texas ranch, and David gave them Texas dancehall billing as "The French Girls." David cut off pieces of steak as he char-grilled it. "I love it hot," he said unapologetically and then confided, "I built that marker just to catch people's attention. They'd think Jesse James or someone like that was buried there. I got the iron grills off an early twentieth-century house that was torn down for the construction of the McAllister Freeway in the 1960s. I knew I'd find some kind of use for them. And you know what? When I put up that historical marker, it stopped every car."

Pleasant Valley

A FRIEND ONCE described the Texas Hill Country as resembling Tuscany. Having spent a good deal of time in Tuscany, I too found the likeness strong: the hills, the stone outcroppings, the small canyons, the cedar brakes, and the scattering of trees—mainly oaks instead of Tuscan olives and cypresses. But above all, both Tuscany and the Hill Country have beautiful, varied grasses that catch the light, the silvery dried stems among the green spring growth. David told me that visitors often say the Hill Country also reminds them of Africa.

While Mary and Margaret and some of my closest friends are passionate about remote landscapes that inspire awe and appear untouched, I've always been much more attracted to the concordance of land and the people who tend to it: nature partly humanized. To my mind, the 5,500 acres at the Bamberger Ranch Preserve are a perfect example of this form of harmony, yet only thirty-seven years earlier, when David first acquired the property, the ranch would have served as a prime example of how human interference can devastate seemingly endless tracts of healthy land and drastically diminish the numbers of animal and plant species that thrive there. As all visitors to the preserve learn, the backdrop of fencing, grass meadows, sculpted cedar brakes, clear running brooks, and hills that form a scalloped horizon was originally the most damaged piece of property in the county, if not in all of the Hill Country.

Much of the surface soil at Selah is whitish caliche—degraded limestone—and in the ravines or on gentler slopes, yellow clay. Dinosaur tracks and marine fossil beds are found on the higher reaches of the ranch, which were once shallow seaside areas during the Cretaceous, when the repeated ebb and flow of the sea created layers of limestone. Most of the rock at

Selah is approximately 100 million years old. However, beneath the Texas Hill Country runs a submerged portion of the Ouachita Mountains that extend up to Arkansas and Oklahoma where they are more visible. These mountains were formed 300 million years ago by tectonic movements, the pressure of a nascent North American continent colliding with a landmass thought to be Africa. The mountains sank into sediment, the eroded materials forming an ever-changing coastline. Along the buried range, we find one of the defining features of the Hill Country, the Balcones Escarpment, a three-hundred mile fault formed by a central Texas uplift, only ten to twenty million years ago—recent in geological time. The fault zone can be seen as a demarcation between fertile flatlands to the east and raised areas to the west, a line that runs from Waco to Austin, passes San Antonio, and turns westward almost to Del Rio in the south. The raised limestone crust wore away, leaving the region's distinctive bluffs, hillsides, and small canyons. Parts of the limestone formations developed cracks, and the subsequent erosion created a system of underground caves and caverns that provide extensive aquifers. The area along the fault became known as the Balcones Escarpment, named by the settlers in the lower eastern lands who thought the hills resembled balconies. Texas writer Stephen Harrigan described the dramatic shift in terrain:

> It is the Balcones that creates the Hill Country, that sets the stage for the Edwards Plateau and the High Plains beyond. The cotton economy, for our schematic purposes, ends at the base of the escarpment, where the rich blackland prairie that sustained the courtly reveries of the old South runs literally into a wall. Above that mass of limestone there is only a veneer of soil, and the country is hard, craggy, and scenic—cowboy country. The distinction is that sharp: farmers to the east, ranchers to the west.

Before describing the astonishing transformation of the ranch land, J. David Bamberger would tell tour groups of the poverty of his early years in rural Ohio. Yet despite the tough 1930s—the enduring depression, his father at times gambling away household money—this sort of poverty in fact offered riches that now seem rare: an appreciation of what nature had to offer to those living near the woods and among pastures. The nineteenth-century romantics would have us believe that nature itself nurtures, that it educates morally and sympathetically. Yes, David's childhood was definitively poor, but his mother, Hester, still took in men who were in wretched shape and broke: traveling the rails and searching out food, shelter, and work. The rails ran below the Bamberger shack. The boys, David and his brothers, were accustomed to this sort of hospitality since Hester, who became a trained nurse, was an intuitive caregiver and an innate lover of the natural world.

"My mother was a total naturalist. She ate nothing that was manufactured. Now you just try that on." David had Hester's welcoming blue eyes. When he had a serious point to make, he had a slight twitch in his left eye that provided a punctuating effect. "But we lived among the Amish people in Ohio, so life as such, eating natural things, didn't seem so unusual. Because we didn't have electricity and running water, Mom kept me and my two brothers outdoors all the time and taught us about the insects, birds, and critters in the grass. She taught us trees, and we planted trees, trees, trees. The J. in my name is for John. My mother said I was like Johnny Appleseed."

No one who knows him doubts that David would put a pot on his head, wear ragged oversized cast-offs, or melt snow with his bare feet for drinking water if he thought for one moment that he could sell something he believed in. Even John Chapman, despite the legendary asceticism of his way of life, was in fact a successful businessman who owned large nurseries in Ohio and Indiana after the territories to the west of Pennsylvania were opened. Some say that the appeal of the apple blossoms around settlers' houses in spring, and of the fruit so well worth preserving, made Chapman's trees a successful commodity. Most children's books don't discuss fermentation or the transcendental powers of spirits. Whatever the connection David's mother made to Johnny Appleseed, such a big part of local Ohio lore, everyone I spoke to, including those who knew David in his youth, confirmed his compulsion to plant trees and later, even more obsessively, to collect their seeds, nurture them, and then plant them by the thousands, often providing sturdy steel fence corrals to protect them for decades from deer, cattle, sheep, and goats. The man who sold vacuum cleaners door-to-door; who as regional manager organized a top sales force of students, housewives, some alcoholics, part-time servicemen, gamblers, men down on their luck, minorities, and immigrants who couldn't speak English; and who finally rose to be co-founder and board chairman of a Fortune 500 fast-food chain—that man was purely and simply nuts about trees. His planting 3,400 trees on Selah alone, and creating an arboretum there, come as no surprise.

The influences that conspired to make David a naturalist were his mother's passion for nature and his early life outdoors. Just by proximity, the natural world and farm life were infused in his soul. His daughter, Deena, who did an extensive family genealogy, insisted that the drive for planting and protecting the natural world was in his genes, carried down from Swiss farming ancestors.

David claimed a third critical influence, in addition to his mother and "Mother Nature," an expression that can sound annoyingly clichéd but one that David insists on using, speaking so often to kids from inner-city schools where "mother" has an array of derogatory senses. Hester, who was a compulsive reader, gave David a copy of Louis Bromfield's *Pleasant Valley,* in which Bromfield, a Pulitzer Prize winner and major Hollywood screenwriter, recounts his return to the farms of his boyhood in northern Ohio. David professed to have read the book eight times, which didn't surprise me. When he and Margaret first became a couple in the mid-1990s, they visited our cramped Paris apartment, where they acted more like lustful adolescents than two mature adults who had three children each, all entering middle age, half with children of their own. These were grandparents making love on the couch while I would try, to no avail, to ignore them, give them privacy, and find some hidden corner in our sixty-five square meters of space. David announced three pilgrimages he intended to make while in Europe: first, to visit a monument just outside Cambridge that listed his brother's name among lost World War II aviators; second, to find his ancestral village in the hills near Bern, Switzerland; and, third, to see Louis Bromfield's former home in Senlis, to the north of Paris. I loaned him our rather shamefully trashed-out Peugeot 205 for that last, sacrosanct experience.

Bromfield was born in Mansfield, Ohio, only forty miles from David's hometown. He grew up believing that he would follow his father's path into farming, but he worked a year on his grandfather's farm, and then studied agriculture, without passion. He began writing for a local newspaper and soon enrolled in Columbia's School of Journalism, where he foundered again until he volunteered for the American Ambulance Corps, joining the 34th and 168th divisions of the French Army in World War I. Bromfield served in seven major battles before returning to the States and journalism. Still fascinated by Europe, he moved with his young family to France, where he began writing novels and short stories, earning high critical praise and then the Pulitzer Prize in 1926 for his third novel, *Early Autumn*. He traveled to places like India, the setting for some of his best-known works, including *The Rains Came*, which was made into an Academy Award-winning film. His main base was the presbytery in Senlis, where he was a passionate gardener. Presbyteries in France are renowned for their *jardins de curé*; these offered not only a calm sanctuary for meditation but also a source of church flowers and of sustenance for the priests themselves, who often lived on modest means.

Bromfield was an astute observer of politics and social trends in Europe, foreseeing its inevitable descent into the darkness and destruction of World War II. He sent his family home to Ohio, and soon afterwards his European friends convinced him that he could do more good for the war effort in the United States than in France.

When the disillusioned Bromfield returned to the States, he sought out his grandparents' farm as a sanctuary. He was dismayed to find the farms he'd known abandoned, the soil "mined" of its nutriments by greedy, uneducated farmers who tried to make a quick profit from over-planting a single cash crop. When the land stopped producing, the farmers moved on to work farms further west or went into local factory work, a pattern that occurred from Ohio to Texas, in large part causing the Dust Bowl.

Bromfield deeply admired French respect for the land: family farms that had remained productive over hundreds of years, the intelligence and care that went into rotating crops and using organic fertilizer. He acquired three farms just south of Mansfield, Ohio, and transformed them into a model for land restoration. He developed a plan whereby a farm would operate almost as a collective, its produce making it self-sufficient, the profits portioned out to workers. He helped design a gorgeous house that fit with traditional rural Ohio architecture but had French detail. He named his farm "Malabar" after India's Malabar Coast.

The more Bromfield employed and wrote about intelligent, profitable land restoration techniques, the more he became known as the world's foremost farmer. He opened up his land to all who were interested in learning. Crowds began frequenting the farm. His nonfiction championed the romantic vision of the mutual nurturing of humans and nature. David said, "Reading that book, *Pleasant Valley*, changed my life. No one before Bromfield talked about 'habitat restoration.' This was well before Rachel Carson and the others. After reading that book, I said to myself that if ever I make money, I want to do the same thing to a piece of land."

Prospects for such environmental heroics seemed pretty remote considering that David arrived in Texas in 1950 with a year-old child, barely a hundred dollars in his pocket, and a résumé that featured door-to-door salesmanship for Airway, a vacuum cleaner company fated to go the way of the mammoth. He had taken up with a competing outfit called Kirby. However, fifty years later, Bamberger was doing exactly what Bromfield did: inviting the public to see, experience, and learn from the vision of a private citizen who with little if any formal training in forestry, botany, or wildlife management had transformed ruined property into a landscape of abundance and diversity. Bamberger and Bromfield preached a similar message: the rewards of—and the ethical responsibility for—good land stewardship are the same whether one owns a 50,000-acre ranch or a postage-stamp sized piece of lawn in the city. But unlike Bromfield, David didn't purchase ruined land by default, but on purpose. He explained, "A real estate broker was taking me around, showing me these fancy homes with landing strips, swimming pools, and tennis courts. And I went, 'No, no, no, you got me all wrong. I want a lousy piece of real estate. I want the worst thing you got. I want something nobody else wants.' The broker looked at me and said, 'Well, there's a whole lot of that around.'"

The fact is that Texans had historically taken poor care of the land, and finding the very worst of it, eventually accumulated in three lots totaling 5,500 acres, was difficult for that very reason: so much of Texas was in bad condition. But once the property was acquired, David called a technician at what was then the Soil Conservation Service (now the Natural Resource Conservation Service, a federal agency) in Johnson City, the county seat, to evaluate the property. He said, "Bamberger, I don't know why you bought it. It will take 43 acres of this land to support one cow. There's not a drop of water. You just bought the worst property in Blanco County."

There wasn't one dependable pond, river, or spring on the first parcel, nearly 3,000 acres, which David purchased in 1969; and the key to success in the development-crazed Texas Hill Country and on the Bamberger Ranch alike was water. The demand for water through suburban sprawl has paved the way for the vast, frightening business of buying and selling water as a commodity, sparking "water wars" across the state. By contrast, the story of water at Selah is affirming, for almost anyone who visits is made to understand that the message is about cherishing and protecting this resource.

In both business and land stewardship, David has operated by a very simple personal rule: "Never start something that you are not prepared to sustain." Like most rules, this one seems self-evident, but the fact is that many ranches fail because the owners lack the will and the know-how to restore and then manage their land. The inconvenience, labor, and costs become overwhelming. Certain family members begin to prefer the city. One unanticipated disaster is followed by another. The critical lesson David took from Bromfield's *Pleasant Valley*, in a chapter titled "The Plan," was that whether you have 10,000 acres or just a half-acre backyard, you have to set clear, achievable goals, have a vision, and stick to it. David tells groups, "Bromfield went to Ohio State University to find people, just like you here today, who were philosophically attuned to his way of thinking. Together they brought the land back. I did the same thing. I hired specialists, and most of them came from Texas A&M University. I don't mean to brag, but I got the best people I could find."

However, the most critical help over the years came from Leroy Petri, who didn't go to A&M but instead served in Vietnam and later built roads and reservoirs for the state of Texas. Except for his stint in the army, Leroy lived his entire life on his parents' farm in Blanco County, not far from Selah. If David could be considered the visionary, Leroy was the hard-working man behind the curtain, the engineer.

In the past, Margaret would have educated tour groups at Selah's arboretum, bat cave, and dinosaur tracks. In fact, she had initiated many of the recent workshops. But during that spring, David gave his blue-eyed squint that meant listen up. "Ordinarily my wife, Margaret, would join us, but she is a cancer patient. She is an excellent geologist, an excellent botanist, and an excellent teacher. She is about the best of everything in the natural world."

Margaret has little tolerance for David's hyperbole. He was the self-described motivator whereas Margaret, the educator, insisted on sticking to facts. She enjoyed making fun of David, telling audiences about a young kid coming up to her after a public tour and asking, "Is everything really the biggest, the best, and the only-est on this ranch?"

On the face of it, Bromfield and David would seem to have little in common. Bromfield was a tall, rugged-looking man who surrounded himself with six largish dogs, all boxers, that he allowed the run of the house. He was a reader and an intellectual, a man steeped in political history and social thinking. He was a celebrity in both literary and Hollywood circles. When he developed Malabar, some critics depicted him as a farmer with a pitchfork in one hand and a cocktail in the other. And while Bromfield preached the power of good farming practices, deeply believing in the Jeffersonian tradition that healthy agriculture was at the very heart of a nation's economy, moral strength, self-sufficiency, and nutritional well-being, he was profligate, overly generous with guests and friends. His experimental farming became outmoded, he planted poor-income crops, and he struggled financially in the end. Malabar and some of its offspring experimental farms failed. Ultimately resurrected by the Ohio State Park system, Malabar serves now as an environmental education center and a tourist attraction, thanks to the famous Bromfield house, but it is all a far cry from the functioning model farm Bromfield had envisioned.

By contrast, David Bamberger was a model of the American rags-to-riches success story, passing through several business incarnations before becoming a staunch spokesman for the environment. He had uncanny instincts and foresight for viable projects, whether in business or land restoration. While Bromfield used his celebrity, charisma, and strong logical appeals, David could sell a vacuum cleaner, a fried chicken store, or environmental conservation to almost anyone, using not only ethics and logic but also the body language and emotional appeals of an evangelical preacher.

Clearly, what Bromfield and David shared more than anything else was a sense of mission, which comes with its own stinging setbacks, losses, and battles above and beyond those allotted in the normal course of life. I had been discussing Bromfield with Jim Berry, the director of The Roger Tory Peterson Institute in Jamestown and former director of Bromfield's Malabar Farm. I told Jim that there was something sad about the Bromfield story. Among other things, he had forsaken his fiction writing, and his environmental message was being lost. Jim said, "He came back from Europe in '39, an expatriate, to the county he was raised in. He had the belief that the health of the country and the world was really in agriculture. That was the basis of everything. Seeing the ecological disaster going on in the United States, starting with the thirties and the Dust Bowl caused by draught and land abuse, he took on a mission. He was trying to change the world, something his fiction wasn't doing."

Jim explained that the survival of environment-minded institutions, generations after their founders have passed away, depends on how fully their original mission remains a part of their identity and is adopted as the passion of subsequent administrators. Unfortunately, Bromfield didn't leave clear instructions for the continuance of Malabar Farm, a mistake David is determined not to make.

When I finally visited Malabar Farm, there wasn't a soul around. The parking lots and roads had black ice, and an arctic wind blew, turning the farm stark and ghostly. It was the day after Pope John Paul II died, and a freak early-April blizzard had hit northern Ohio. The day of the storm, I had dropped by to see Don and Donna Airhart, close friends of David's who still lived in Navarre, his childhood town. Malabar was only an hour away at most, and I thought I could catch a late tour of the big house and still make some afternoon progress on the road to Texas. But snow and wind struck with unnerving ferocity, and the snow grew so deep so quickly that I couldn't control the car. At three in the afternoon, after poring over my guide to "dog-friendly" accommodations, I found myself checking into a motel where the telephones were out and half the heating in the building was non-functional. Feeling trapped, I began drinking some Labatts and turned on the television to watch world reactions to Pope John Paul II's death. The snowfall seemed preposterously heavy in the parking lot and a Shamrock gas station barely visible out my window. Snowbell and Pandora were thrilled to escape the car, chasing each other over the twin beds. I started writing in my notes: "Maybe Bromfield wants me to slow down and pay attention."

David would concur with this sentiment, albeit in a slightly differ-ent context. Selah, the name of his ranch preserve, is based on slowing down and paying attention, as he often explains. "I took five years of Bible studies. I noticed in the Old Testament, in the Book of Psalms, the word *selah* appears seventy-one times, often at the end of a passage. It occurs when a significant statement has been made, and a moment is needed, a stop. They think it comes from a musical term meaning 'pause and reflect.' To me, Selah is what Walden Pond is to Thoreau."

Hes' Country Store

. . . .

I HAVE AN image of J. David Bamberger that I'm still unable to shake, partly because of the situation that produced it but mostly because at that moment it became clear to me that he was incapable of doing anything without flair. A small procession of family members had climbed Setulah Mountain in Highlands, North Carolina, to toss the ashes of Dr. Thomas B. Crumpler, Mary and Margaret's father, thus David's and my mutual father-in-law, off a stunning granite cliff that looks out over Nantahala National Forest, just south of the Great Smoky Mountain range. Family members had taken modest handfuls of pale, sandy ash and made respectful, although rather unsuccessful, attempts to toss the ashes against the wind. David went last, taking the can itself and shouting out, "Damn it, we're gonna miss you, Professor Crumpler." He whipped the can in the air, trying to propel the ashes cliff-ward, the ashes catching the wind like a pale wing and flying right back over us, all of us holding our breaths as David kept hurling ashes and wavering at the cliff's edge, Margaret shouting, "Get back, David!" But no, he was in the act of paying tribute, and this was his stage even if it did have a thousand-foot drop. We worried that we were going to see something truly unusual: a fatal accident at a funeral. What is not unusual is for a Bamberger to make an abrupt end.

During family gatherings in Highlands, I became entranced by David's descriptions of Selah and his projects and ambitions for the preserve that I had yet, at that time, to see. Also it was in Highlands, many years earlier, that Margaret volunteered in her spare time at the Highlands Biological Station. She illustrated the center's catalog and began to train herself in botany and ornithology. She claims that these were her first substantial steps to becoming a naturalist. Remarkably, soon after meeting David, she was already transforming Selah's workshops into what would become award-winning educational programs.

Setulah became a family meeting place between Texas and Paris, and the reverence David showed our father-in-law was moving. Both men delighted in stories, and between the two these flowed fast, with escalating embellishment and theatrics. David managed to extract stories that even the daughters hadn't heard, stories of their grandfather, his failed crops in Alabama, his futile oil drilling in Texas, his mixed success as a retailer in Virginia. I would learn later that David would preach not only nature conservation but also the conservation of family heritage. He exhorted middle-school kids on free lunch programs and privileged private school students alike to call their grandparents and listen to their stories, absorb their experiences and knowledge while they still had the chance, and take pride in family history, however modest. He did no less with Dr. Crumpler.

On Selah, David had constructed a peculiar shrine to his mother, which he named Hes' Country Store. Like the site of the historical marker, the building was a compilation of recycled materials. David recovered planks from old Mexican shacks at a west-side San Antonio urban renewal site, the contractor saying, "Take all you want." David used window frames and doors that he recovered from the famed Hill Country birthplace of Admiral Nimitz, a property in Fredericksburg that David bought and restored, receiving a Texas historical classification. The final, more ornate fittings came from a salvage lot called Used House Parts. Hes' Country Store was filled with objects that belonged to his mother and to the epoch of his youth. A replica of an original Texas country store, it bore little resemblance to David's childhood home. Still, you couldn't avoid infusing it into your imaginings of his childhood, and the array of objects was a proper reflection of Hester's penchant for finding, collecting, and even hoarding things to the point that her home verged on chaos. David's first wife, Donna, who adored Hester, described Hester's housekeeping: "Housekeeping was not her forte. The kitchen was clean but cluttered; the rest of the house was a mess. There were magazines, newspapers and clippings, books, stationery, birds' nests and feathers, sewing tools and quilt scraps, sweaters, scarves, shoes, soil, seeds, jars, bric-a-brac, and dozens of other things I can't recall lying on the floor, chairs, or shelves and even on top of each other."

In his shrine or "museum," as he described it, David allowed for a collection of objects, particularly those that evoked the 1930s. While David is not fastidious, he clearly is Hes' opposite when it comes to order and cleanliness. He has an aesthetic sense that extends to the buildings he designs and to the landscape itself. He maintains the depot for recyclable materials well out of sight of visitors. He washes dishes and counters, using diluted soap when possible to avoid waste and unnecessary expense.

Hester's shrine turned out to be lucrative, costing a mere $10,000 to build and used as both a hunting cabin and his podium for family heritage conservation. In addition, David can capitalize on the emotional appeal of his mother's story when it is delivered on the porch between a bleached deer skull with its eight-point rack and a presiding cigar-store Indian.

Of the photographs I've seen of David Bamberger—and there are many, particularly in journals and magazines—the one that I like most, and the most telling in its own way, was taken in March 1936 when he was only seven. He is standing with his two older brothers. Jim, on the left, is almost twice as tall as David on the right and at least a head taller than Tom in the middle. In a dress shirt and tie, Jim drapes his arm comfortably over Tom's shoulder while looking earnestly at the camera, if only because of the bright sunlight. Tom is wearing knickers, striped socks pulled up just below the knees, a crewneck sweater obscuring his tie. He is standing at relaxed attention, his eyes closed, though he is obviously amused, trying to contain a smile. However, neither boy seems to be enjoying the moment as much as David, in a dark stocking cap and, in contrast to his more formally dressed brothers, denim overalls torn at the left knee, his head hunched defensively as he holds up two fists ready to box the photographer. In all probability, Hester took the shot with Jim's Brownie box camera, for which that year's ad campaign was, "Childhood, like Christmas, is gone before you know it." David was already a showman.

On tours of Selah, David simplifies the story of his early years; he wants his audience to understand that he inherited nothing, that while growing up in the tough depression years in a shack without utilities he profited from the tutelary influences of surrounding farms and woods, his mother's passion for gardening, and her fanatical love of nature. The rural community itself was populated with poor people who were hard-working and colorful. His not-so-veiled message is that inherited wealth and social position are poison since they are achieved through neither initiative nor ingenuity and often lead to waste and insensitivity. David instinctively shapes his story to build ethos.

But the real Ohio story is far more striking than he lets on and fits a larger cultural/historical picture of America. One envisions his family living in a raw wooden shack near the Amish farms outside Navarre, a small community on the Ohio Canal, southwest of Canton. But the family didn't move to Navarre until the year before the photograph of the brothers was taken. David's earliest years were spent at 1120 Wallace Avenue in a middle-class neighborhood in Massillon. This part of northern Ohio was in the steel belt, which included eastern Ohio, West Virginia, and western Pennsylvania. Later, with the demise of the industry due to foreign competition, some of which the Marshall Plan had facilitated, the area became known as the Rust Belt. Massillon was the home of one of Republic Steel's vast plants. Employing as many as 6,700 workers in its mills and on the extensive yards, Republic was the dark monolith of the local economy, its hellish open-hearth furnaces destined for extinction.

David remembers little of the Massillon house, torn down now, or the early days in town except for the trauma of losing his dog Blacky, his father explaining that Blacky was "gone." David saw Blacky in the garage, and couldn't reconcile "gone" with "dead." He also lost his friend Jacky to pneumonia and, again misunderstanding, shouted to him as he and other neighbor kids often did from Jacky's yard to come out and play, only to find that he was "gone" too.

Bamberger names were traditionally picked out of the Bible, the Book of Titus being the origin of David's father's name Titus, and as if life weren't confusing enough, sons were called by their father's name. The boys were called Titus the way their friends the Netzlys were all called Charley after their father. Titus the father was surprisingly aristocratic looking, with fine features, though he made a living first as a Pennsylvania Railroad clerk, then as an automobile salesman for Hudson Terraplanes and Essex. During the war, when car sales evaporated, he was forced to work as a uniformed security guard for the grounds at Union Drawn Steel, another plant in town. Hester had come to Ohio from Indiana after reading that the Massillon Hospital, because of a shortage of nurses during the First World War, was recruiting and training nurses who did not have degrees. She had not progressed beyond the eighth grade and yet breezed through her boards to become a registered nurse. The nurse trainees would learn and develop their healthcare instincts from hands-on experience, and the young women working together formed bonds that would last their whole lives. Their pictures are preserved in the Massillon Historical Museum. However, Hester would leave nursing to become a housewife for more than a decade after marrying Titus Bamberger and bearing three boys.

David was born on June 11, 1928, a year and four months before the New York Stock Exchange's Black Thursday. As most Americans know, particularly David's generation, the sell-off on October 24, 1929 triggered a decline in stock prices that wouldn't bottom out until 1932. The market dropped 89% percent of its value, from 386 to 40.46, and didn't regain its pre-crash level until the early 1950s. Production fell by more than half, and unemployment rose to nearly 30%. Industrial regions such as northern Ohio were particularly hard-hit. Money became so scarce that the government closed banks and desperately printed money, using plates dating back to the Civil War, stocking selected banks during the night and then reopening them.

Titus Bamberger managed to provide for his family during the 1930s, working alternately seven-day and six-day weeks, coming home late and leaving in the morning so that the boys rarely saw him. Tom described him as a "rounder," an out-of-date expression fitting the times. He wasn't an alcoholic, exactly, but he made the rounds of bars and women and was an obsessive gambler, all of which precipitated some impassioned moments, with Hester letting chairs fly or making other not-so-subtle gestures of disapproval.

One might deduce a disparaging portrait of Bamberger as a father, but the boys saw just the opposite. While certainly not always responsible, he was a hard-working, resourceful man whose family in Massillon provided a supportive network of aunts, uncles, and cousins. The boys were thrilled when he had a day at home, every second Sunday.

Tom and David were audacious from the start, loving humor and storytelling. They became exceptional poker players, a skill that would get them through some financial scrapes. Tom began reading classic novels at ten; David became the country boy with boundless energy and a nascent love of farms and woods. The oldest brother, Jim, was different; he was solemn and chaste, and he unselfishly took on some of the responsibilities of man of the house and supported Hes emotionally, Titus being all but absent. Tom would say of Jim, "If ever there was a person pure at heart, he was it. He went to Sunday school and believed all that. He was going to be a preacher." Even now in the family, when Jim's name comes up, the tone of the conversation shifts to veneration. Hes, above all, adored him.

David took me up to Tahlequah, Oklahoma, the capitol of the Cherokee Nation, to spend time with Tom on his ranch, situated along the clear Baron Fork Creek, rich in wildlife: bald eagles and vultures floating above and gar, bass, turtles, and water snakes packed in together below the bank. At nearly 80, Tom was still serving as a substitute judge.

I asked both Tom and David if Hester's parents had fostered her love of the natural world, and David responded, "She didn't have much parents."

Tom said, "She had Bert. Remember Bert? Now, there's a character."

"But he put her in a Methodist orphans' home."

"Hey, do you remember the time Bert took us to the railroad track to see Herbert Hoover?"

"Oh, yeah."

"Who was Bert?" I asked.

"Our grandfather Bert was a German glassblower who lived in Indiana. He hated the Democrats because some guy during the Wilson administration invented a machine that could blow glass better and cheaper than he could and he was out of work and never held a job after that. He blamed the Democrats. God knows why. He was a beer drinker, and we loved when he visited us because he'd leave all those bottles, and we'd fill the wagon and get that one-cent deposit on them. He'd leave fifty beer bottles. He read in the paper where President HOOO-VER (he always emphasized the name) was coming through town on the train. There wasn't one other person who liked Hoover in those days, but Bert loved Herbert Hoover, even looked a little bit like him. Red-faced and bald-headed, you know. He said, 'Boys, tomorrow is going to be the greatest day in your life. I'm taking you to the train station to see President HOOO-VER!' That day we dressed up in our Sunday knickers and he gave each of us a dime. He said, 'Put these dimes on the track when President Hoover's train passes over it, and you will have something to remember; you can make it into a bracelet. Tell your children the flattened dime bracelet was made by President HOOO-VER's train.' Well, we palmed the dimes, of course, just pretended to put them on the track. That was too much money to have run over. But you know our other grandfather, Louis Henry Bamberger, was hit by a train right at that very spot. First police officer killed in the line of duty in Massillon. They always said he was chasing a crook down the track, but I heard that he was standing on the tracks talking to some guy and the Twentieth Century Limited came through and that damned train didn't slow down for anybody."

I learned that grandfather Louis's brother, Albert Bamberger, was the first fireman killed in the line of duty in Massillon when a wall of the Russell & Company Plant collapsed on him in flames. Years later the town decided to honor the two notable civil servants who had given their lives while serving their community, but officials couldn't figure out where their graves were and made no special effort to find them.

Hester must have developed an independent spirit at an early age: her mother, Cora, died of tuberculosis when she was seven; her father put her for a time in the care of a Methodist minister. She tended to exaggerate having been an orphan, since Bert remarried—a woman named Effie—and they did care for her. Later, raising three boys must have been a handful for Hester, and when she had to, she became fierce and righteous, particularly if men coming through trying to make a buck were swindling the boys. She'd march over to the seediest parts of town to recover fifty cents, even, if it rightly belonged to the kids. She was a small woman with blue eyes, and attractive, though she had a pronounced nose, a trait genetically superseding Titus's finer ones and providing the boys with a family look. You could tell a Bamberger boy just by the shape of his nose.

Titus moved his family to the country because all three boys had asthma. Massillon was a steel town: belching black smoke, soot exacerbated by coal furnaces in every house. Two hours after a snow, a black crust formed. Titus bought the farm for $800, and the cleaner air worked. The boys' asthma virtually ceased.

The so-called farm consisted of two acres of field, two of woods, and a small creek. The house had been constructed by pushing two shacks together. They began to separate during the family's first winter, which happened to be one of the worst on record. Snow accumulations mounted higher than the kids' heads; cold and flurries drifted through the split in the shacks. Hester injured her eye while chopping wood and was bedridden. The injury would later cause a cataract. The boys, unused to the country, suddenly found themselves taking over all of the responsibilities, the older boys chopping and splitting wood, little David collecting the chips for kindling. They made the meals, heated the house, and looked after the animals. David fetched water from the nearest well, at the Jones's place a quarter mile up the road.

With the help of the Airharts, nearly lifelong friends of David's who lived in Navarre, I visited Crossroads. There was snow on the ground, and the trees were stripped, with no signs of spring. I was not far from where the picture of the Bamberger boys was taken on a sunny day, with a road and slope like the ones where I walked with my own camera. But unbeknownst to me at the time, the blizzard was just a half-hour away, the first flakes falling while I was trying to take photographs of the shack, raising the suspicions of a neighbor. Pandora and Snowbell, eager to inspect the yard and run down to the tracks, were not helping. This area was hardly glitzy, the yards muddied and the pastures empty. I imagined carrying water in winter, trying to heat the house with firewood, and doing homework with insufficient light and endless distractions. On every comparative count, Hes' Country Store at Selah was luxurious.

The Cistern

YOU CAN SEE in practice at Selah more than sixty years later the glimmerings of social and ecological principles by which the Bamberger family lived: hospitality, recycling, growing their own food, and the innovative collection of water. Hester instilled the values of industriousness and frugality while training the boys to plant trees, recognize the different birds and insects, identify plants, and look after the garden. This also resulted in some wacky secret experiments, such as trying to grow the world's largest pumpkin by boring a small hole in it and nurturing the gourd on milk. If a pumpkin can fatten a cow, why not milk a pumpkin? The results were not satisfactory. Years later David would be doing breeding experiments on cattle and devising programs for saving endangered species.

When David teaches at Selah, he always conjures his years at Crossroads, usually in the form of stories that personalize the importance of human and environmental heritage. These stories often take the form of fables and he projects a humility that appeals to his audience but downplays the complexity of the times and how exceptional Hester really was. I visited the one-room schoolhouse the Bamberger boys attended, a converted brick Grange Hall that still stands next to the Crossroads Union Cemetery, open to the edge of Elton Street SW and containing some rather large granite monuments. On the corner of Elton and Pigeon Run Road stands the stark, white Saint James United Church of Christ, with a single bell visible in its steeple. The school consisted of a small auditorium with a stage. The students ranged from first to eighth graders. David, the only first grader, was nicknamed Cub by the upper-grade girls. When I talked to his high-school friends from Navarre and his ex-wife Donna Bamberger, whose family goes back five generations in Navarre, they invariably referred to him as Cub or Cubbie. In a way, it was a privilege to be the youngest in a school where the studies were for more advanced grades. David used antics and showmanship to keep his older classmates amused over the three years before his and several other small schools were consolidated in the nearby town of Justus.

Hes' photograph of the three boys was taken at the end of their first winter. Since she was taking photographs, Hester's eye must have healed, and soon she would be preparing organic garden beds. They already had a calf. That same day Hester took another photograph of Tom and David standing beside the calf, which was tied to a still-dormant tree. Soon Titus was bringing home cows, horses, goats, and pigs for the family to take care of. Who knows how he acquired them: bets, cards, or simply paying five or ten dollars? The small farm may not have had utilities, but with Hester's know-how and the boys doing chores it soon produced an abundance of food. Their cow alone could supply an army with rich milk, cheese, and yogurt. The boys trapped muskrats, skunks, raccoons, and even mink to sell their hides, and they hunted rabbit and birds for meals. Money was so tight that they felt the sting when shotgun shells at the Justus general store went from five to ten cents.

The house was situated only a few hundred yards from the crossing of the Wheeling and Lake Erie and the Baltimore & Ohio railroads, where a signalman lived in a house the size of a small latrine. Every train was required to stop and blow its whistle, making sure that the crossing was clear. The crossing was dangerous: once, coming home from a bar, Titus bailed out of his car and nearly derailed a B & O.

When the trains stopped at the crossing, the bums riding the rods would jump off the freight cars. They were called bums or hoboes, but in fact they were just young, energetic men looking for work, any kind of work, and freight was the only way they could travel. When they jumped off the trains, the farm with Hes and three little kids was the first place they came to. They were always fed, and some slept in the barn; some stayed for weeks, helping out.

Hes was by nature compelled to help the poor and downtrodden, even giving food to needy townspeople if they could get out to the country. After the Wagner Act allowed workers to organize for collective bargaining and the AFL and later the CIO were formed, bitter strikes hit the steel industry. U.S. Steel and Bethlehem worked out agreements with employees, but the management in companies known as "Little Steel," Republic Steel in particular, dominated workers by hiring Pinkerton guards and mobilizing the police to bully demonstrators. A year after the photograph of the boys was taken and two years after the family left Massillon, police fired on strikers, killing three and wounding numerous others.

Meanwhile, Bamberger hospitality on the farm was rewarded with outside news, which was scarce in Amish country. They'd hear intriguing stories about and descriptions of states such as Alabama, Mississippi, and Arkansas. One young traveler named Curtis stayed for a month. He was an early riser, the type who was clever and had to keep busy. He insisted on working for his board, and the project he took on was to devise a collection system to bring drinking water to the farm.

Water for the animals and washing came from a hole dug in the farmyard, but it wasn't usable in the household. Curtis started by constructing a cistern, digging fifteen feet into the ground beside the house. The boys contributed by descending into the hole on a ladder and hauling out buckets of dirt. Titus brought sacks of concrete for the encasement, and Curtis then hooked up spouting to the tin roof of the shack. He installed a small crank device to the piping that allowed a runoff of the first rainwater, washing soot and dirt from the roof. When the water ran clear, it would be diverted into the cistern. Once Titus had bought and mounted a hand pump, the system ran with remarkable efficiency. Rainwater collection is at least as old as civilization itself. The cisterns in ruins of former Crusader castles in Jordan still provide water for the local populations. Curtis, using native ingenuity, radically improved the quality of life on the little Ohio farm, and Titus was so pleased that he brought Curtis to his Uncle Oscar, who was then head of the rolling mill at Republic Steel. Curtis got a job.

The Bamberger boys would do anything to earn change. They collected wild strawberries, blackberries, and sassafras and sold packets of these at the car dealership where their father worked. When the trains stopped, they'd board the coal cars, toss off handfuls of coal, and then collect it in burlap bags. They'd scour people's dumps for discarded aluminum and collect zinc lids from mason jars. They even spent weeks amassing steel that came off trains: brake shoes and steel parts. They thought they'd make a fortune selling it in bulk to be recycled. Butch, a heavy-set Jewish man, would come to buy the scrap metal. He said, "Boys, I'll take the aluminum and zinc, but you're going to have to haul that steel back to the tracks. I can't take it. It's illegal." It never occurred to the boys what would become of the American railroad system if its steel could be sold for scrap. Hester often invited Butch to dinner, the family impatient for the latest news, while Butch nurtured futile hopes of somehow winning Hester's heart.

Hester couldn't live without a garden, and she loved both the Amish people and the local farmers. People would say to her, "You live at Crossroads. You farmers?" She'd reply, "No, we're not smart enough," a clear echo of Bromfield's belief that farming, of all professions, requires the broadest knowledge and receptivity: "He has to be a biologist, a veterinarian, a mechanic, a botanist, a horticulturist, and many other things, and he has to have an open mind, eager and ready to absorb new knowledge and new ideas and new ideals."

Rural life created a sense of community with thrashing, canning, quilting, butchering, festivals, school activities, and church life. This support system is something that David promotes with the families who live and work on Selah. However, boys, particularly in those days, took the community and their housewife mothers for granted; only many years later would Hester be truly appreciated. The boys were anxious to prove themselves at an early age. At Crossroads, David kept a pony and, a natural horseman, rode everywhere he could. Titus bought horses, igniting further tension between himself and Hester, who felt that the household priorities were being ignored. Paradoxically, such irresponsibility only enhanced the bond between David and his father, since they loved to ride together, work hours permitting. David recalled, "This is hard to say, because I was so young. But I was probably his favorite son, mostly because I had the little pony and I'd ride him when Dad went on horseback. I rode him with a bridle. I never had a saddle, never owned one. I knew how to hold on to the mane of a horse. I remember being up in someone's barnyard. Here in Texas we call it a corral, but up there it's a big barn, a haystack, and a fenced yard. It was always boards; it wasn't wire. This guy brought out a young horse, and there was discussion that went on between the adults. I remember my dad saying 'Well, this boy can ride him.' He asked me if I was willing, and I said, 'Yeah.' I think they were taking bets. And they had a rope on the horse that went around his head and his muzzle. I wouldn't have been ten. My dad threw me up on the horse, and I grabbed the mane, and that horse let loose as soon as my body hit his back. And I mean he bucked. All the men ran for the fences, and my dad kinda stayed out there because he felt maybe I'd get thrown. I remember going up where my whole body left that horse while I was still holding the mane. I'd come back down on that horse and go up again. It was just like a jack-in-the-box. Anyway, that dammed horse, after doing that for about a minute, decided he couldn't throw me off, and he stopped. I'm scared to death. I know that much. I'm looking around, and my dad had his hand out, and he was collecting them dollar bills. He told me as we rode on to the next place, 'You did a good job, Davy.'"

Of course, the moment became mythic for a ten-year-old and is enlightening when one considers the challenges David would later relish. As simplistic as it may sound, telling David that a thing couldn't be done amounted to waving a red cape at him. Most of us have our rite-of-passage stories, often more remarkable ones, but when David told me about his father betting on his breaking the horse a different sort of poignancy struck me. Despite the depression years, his early childhood was in many ways idyllic, Wordsworthian. Living outdoors, he would intuitively believe, with the poet, "that Nature never did betray / The heart that loved her," but he couldn't have guessed then that his fierce mission in later life would be to change the hearts of those who betrayed nature. Nor would he have guessed that in a few short years, his world and everyone else's would so radically change.

It broke his heart when the family moved back to Massillon as finances grew tight. David brought his pony to the city and built a stable onto the side of the garage. But it was impossible to keep a pony in a small yard. He was forced to move the pony to the stables out of town where his father's horse was kept. Hester couldn't reconcile the family's owning and boarding horses when there wasn't enough money for a washing machine. She had to boil water in a tub to do laundry by hand. Titus's compulsive gambling only made matters worse.

Back in Massillon, the boys were the hardest-working kids in town. David swept the barber shop, cleaned windows, cut grass in the cemetery, delivered the *Evening Independent* as a substitute paper boy, and bought old bicycles for two or three dollars and fixed them up to resell. Often he and his brothers were sent two hundred and fifty miles away to Hartford City, Indiana, to spend the summers with their aunt and uncle. Even there, they'd sell vegetables door-to-door. All of the boys did well in school. David took up the trumpet and played in both junior high and later in high school while Tom played football for perennial state champs Massillon High.

On October 22, 1942, David was in algebra at Longfellow Junior High School, and his teacher was named, of all things, Anna Bamberger. Longfellow was on the route to the Massillon City Hospital. That warm autumn morning suddenly filled with "just sirens and sirens and sirens," as David described it. He sat as did the rest of the class, unable to hear the teacher. It was the moment of his father's accident. His father, by then a security guard, was patrolling the steelyard when an overloaded crane boom buckled, dropping its load. The steel crushed Titus from the waist down. An adult appeared in the classroom and led David away while the other students sat puzzled. He was taken to Hester and then the hospital. David remembered, "My dad was in a death situation. I saw him for only a moment, just long enough for him to say one thing: 'Listen to your mother.'"

Soon after, the family came apart. Jim, who was already at Elmhurst College in Illinois studying to become a minister, enlisted in the air corps and became a B-26 bombardier in the 9th Air Force, flying missions out of the Earls Colne base in England.

I was walking with David on the Rachel Carson Trail at Selah, where he was checking on preparations for a tour, pruning shears in hand. His motto is "Never go out on the land without a tool." David often talks while lopping off overgrowth on the path, sweeping out dinosaur tracks, and even cleaning the toilet at the ranch office near the George Beere Greenhouse. He stopped and turned to me, his eyes the same blue as Hes', and confessed, "I wasn't good to Mom. She needed me, and I was young and full of myself. But what I did do was write to the governor of Ohio, saying my father was killed in the steelyard and one brother was in the service and the other outside the household. 'My mother can't drive and I'd like to apply for a driver's license so that I can help her get to town.'" The Joneses had a 1928 Chevrolet soft-top coupe, which they gave to Hes, and David would sit in the front seat practicing the motions of driving. He knew that he could drive. The governor wrote back that if David could pass the driving test, he could obtain a license, albeit one restricted to necessities. At fourteen, David acquired a license with the following statement printed on it: "Valid for driving back and forth to school and taking his mother to the grocery." He obtained extra gas tickets from a girlfriend of Jim's who worked in the rationing office.

Hes was, in the end, compensated $44,000 by Union Steel for Titus's death and received social security for herself and David. She bought a small three-floor house and 30 acres less than a half-mile from the shack at Crossroads, and she eventually returned to nursing at the Massillon Hospital. She also took in a friend from nurse training along with her husband, who had also been injured in an industrial accident. In a way, Hes had been liberated by her own husband's death; she was independent-minded and smart and despite her loneliness wouldn't consider

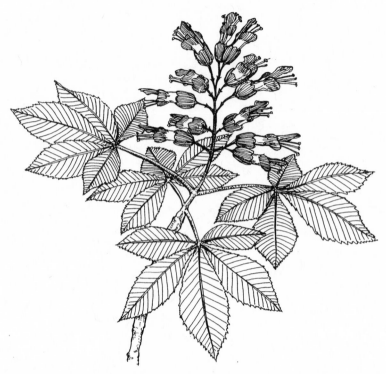

RED BUCKEYE *Aesculus pavia*

remarrying. She undoubtedly worried about David's values, imagining that he might turn out like his father. She scolded David for writing a dollar sign on the bathroom mirror with his shaving brush and cream. It left an odd, ghostly mark. David shouted back, "I'm not going to be poor."

Hes had a particular fondness for Jim, who had been training to be a minister. Jim couldn't have been more different from his father and gave Hes comfort when there were family conflicts. He wrote to his brothers, sending young David pictures of flak from anti-aircraft artillery fire and of the crew—Jerome St. Peter, Sergeant Neal, Staff Sergeant Thibult, and Johnson—assembled under the nose of their B26 Wolf Pack II. Jim sent V-mail: photographed versions of letters he'd write.

Adoring his Army Air Corps brother, David became an expert in every imaginable aircraft in the war. Hes forbade him to listen to the radio at night since he had to go to school. David listened to the teardrop-shaped radio anyway, the volume just audible, and heard that Jim's 9th Air Force had launched a bombing mission against Dieppe. He had flown over forty missions and had himself predicted that he would never return from Europe. David knew that night in a telepathic way that his brother had been shot down. He told his mother the next day that the 9th Air Force had been engaged in a major offensive. Ten days later two military officials came to Crossroads to announce that Jim was missing in action.

The family received reports that the Wolf Pack II had been damaged and had fallen out of formation to return to England. One of the gunners washed up on the English coast. Jim's disappearance devastated Hester. Despite overwhelming evidence that Jim had died when the Wolf Pack II plunged into the English Channel, she spent her life expecting him to show up at the door. That is the cruelty of missing-in-action. There is no finality to it, Jim's flight endless in Hes' imagination and heart.

Jacob's Ladder

IN THE EARLY 1970s, David and Donna joined a Bible study group that focused on the Old Testament. The restoration of the ranch was well under way. His studies had already given him the word "Selah," and like Adam, he could begin assigning names in his own paradise. Among many bucolic spots on Selah, one is particularly beautiful. It has a lovely, clear pool and trails rising over a small, wooded canyon, all less than a half-mile from the ranch house. It's little wonder that in the early days David would bring friends there to sit on the rocks and discuss business, politics, and philosophy—a laidback, Texas version of Socratic dialogues. At the site, only a trickle ran in the creek bed as water was returning to the newly restored land, and David envisioned a series of ladders that would connect the big stone outcroppings so that you could walk to the top of the hill. While Jacob dreamed of a ladder on which angels commuted between heaven and earth, David saw steps up to a perfect specimen of a Texas madrone tree. Madrones were relatively rare on the overgrazed ranch. At first, he found only five on 5,500 acres, but he would later find several dozen others and plant fifty more in canyons where cedar had been cut and left on the ground. David had an affection for them, not only because they add much-needed biodiversity but also because they are, with their clusters of white, lantern-shaped flowers, reddish berries, evergreen leaves and smooth, apricot-tinted bark, trees for all seasons. Leroy constructed a cement dam with a low-water crossing on the creek. The name David gave to the place was, of course, Jacob's Ladder.

David experienced several professional incarnations while ascending the career ladder before finally creating what Michael Murphy would call "Hill Country Heaven" in his *Texas Highways* article. The climb was anything but stable or predictable. You might even say rungs were missing. Still, David had particular gifts that would serve him well over the long haul. Donna readily pointed out two: "Cub has always been able to find the best people to work for him, and no one else can come up with a sales angle like he can." David himself would say to me without a glimmer of modesty, "Hell, to be plain honest with you about it, I could just foresee stuff when other folks had no idea." Still, despite these combined advantages, David experienced no shortage of foolish disasters, unprompted adventures, and wild successes graced by dumb luck.

I visited Donna several times. It was more than ten years after her divorce from David, and she now lived on the west side of San Antonio in a gated community that comes with all the trappings: courteous guards, meticulous landscaping, jogging and bike paths, and sports facilities. It also had a resident population of deer that no one wanted but that by law couldn't be gotten rid of: No one could shoot them within city limits.

For both David and Donna, the divorce was not free of bitterness and depression, but after forty-five years of marriage they were still able to settle without court battles that would beget additional acrimony. Remarkably, after a suspicious start, Donna became one of Margaret's greatest fans. She said bluntly, "Margaret has given that ranch its credibility. It didn't have those education programs until she came along."

Donna looked much younger than her seventy-seven years. Her eyes a warm brown, her comments always self-effacing, she was quick to laugh and shake her head incredulously over family adventures. I flipped through family photo albums while she spoke. "I was so gullible. Cub could talk me into anything." Donna kept her attractive house spotless, every wall tastefully covered with quality paintings that were almost exclusively still-lifes and landscapes, the anomaly being a sumptuous nude hanging in her bedroom. She became a passionate collector after David bought her her first landscape. He would later commission for Donna's birthday not only the painter's work but also a delivery by the artist himself. Her bureau had a collection of colorful stones, shells, and other natural objects found on various ranches that she and David owned.

Donna's family dated back in Navarre to pre-Civil War days, the old Nichols Farm coming to the family via the nineteenth-century Land Grant Program. They were modest, hardworking farmers with a family secret: Her grandfather was conceived in an out-of-wedlock Civil War romance, the great-grandmother silently bearing the stigma. The fact that Donna's father wouldn't speak of it two generations later only intensified the intrigue and underscored the strait-laced values of rural Ohio.

Donna had a neighbor in Navarre, Margaret-Jean, six years older, who with two sisters rented a cabin each year on Turkeyfoot Lake, just twenty miles north, near Akron. Turkeyfoot is a part of the natural Portage Lakes, which were important to the Indians and then to the early pioneers in the area. For locals, the Portage Lakes, their name deriving from the portage path between rivers, provided reservoirs and summer enchantment. Margaret-Jean's sisters invited their friends, Donna among them. In the middle of the two weeks, one of the girls, Mary, had to return home and asked to go on a last rowboat ride. Donna volunteered to go with her, each taking an oar, and on the lake, as if conjured, a canoe materialized with two sixteen-year-old boys, one of whom was Mary's classmate. She only had to shout out, "Hi, Bob!" and the canoe veered purposefully their way. Donna recalled, "There was this cute guy with a crew cut. He had on Air Force sunglasses that were all the rage. Right then I fell for him. I was just smitten."

The same year that the Wolf Pack II fell from the sky over the English Channel, breaking Hes' heart—and everyone else's for that matter—David's high school sweetheart was delivered unto him by water. They had met on July 3, 1944, when in Europe the Allies were consolidating forces and fighting hedge to hedge in Normandy, looking to break out across France. On that Ohio lake, with its cabins, rowboats, and fireflies, hearts were in tumult, and by late summer David chose to enroll in Navarre High School with the sole purpose of pursuing Donna Beem.

That winter David invited Donna out to Crossroads to sled, and she met Hester for the first time. She'd never before encountered anyone quite like her, an independent spirit, a naturalist, and an avid reader. Most women in Donna's sphere, herself included, aspired to become dedicated homemakers. Order and cleanliness were incontestable laws of American family life, and Hester represented bedlam. Hester stood up to authority whenever she thought it fit, countering doctors' advice by treating her own ailments or defying a hospital director by inviting a black nurse to a weekend picnic. When told, "We work with blacks and treat them fair, but we don't socialize with them," Hes responded, "Well, we are going to socialize with them at my house." Later, Donna would regret not having been closer to Hester, but their sensibilities differed radically. It took decades of tolerance and sympathy on both sides before they would deeply value each other's company.

David's business aspirations followed an evolutionary course, from fixing up old bicycles for resale to doing the same with automobiles. Every Saturday or Sunday morning, he would drive to Canton, buy the paper for a dime, and scan the classifieds for bargains. Sometimes he would see an antique car sitting neglected in a shed or with grass growing up around it in a yard. He'd haggle with a farmer for it and then engage the talents of schoolmate and mechanical whiz Richard Telarico to get the car fired up. David cleaned, painted, and then sold the cars, giving Telarico a cut of the profits. David had entered his father's domain, albeit the cottage industry version, selling used cars out of Hes' driveway. The business flourished until he received a letter from the state inquiring about his dealer's license and sales tax. The existence of such legal impediments had never entered David's mind.

Fortunately, when he was forced out of business, it was only weeks before his graduation and his enlistment in the army. The war was over, but the draft was still on. He calculated that one way or another he'd be forced into the military. He signed up for the shortest possible stretch, eighteen months in the army, and shipped with his mother's dictum ringing in his ears: "Keep yourself clean mentally, physically, and morally," which he interpreted abstractly until the military showed films depicting the unpleasantness of syphilis and gonorrhea.

Nothing could have suited David's disposition less than army life. He had grown up a wild kid, his father basically absent and the only consistent authority being Hester, who was an eccentric by most standards. He was first sent to Fort Belvoir, Virginia, for basic training, and then to Carlisle Barracks, the historic war college located ironically in Quaker country, just southwest of Harrisburg, Pennsylvania. After the industrial-age world wars of the first half of the twentieth century, the school adapted to the Cold War era in which the slant and dissemination of information were strategic in and of themselves. David trained as an Information and Education Specialist and attended orientations every Monday morning, where officers sorted through a collection of newspapers, instructing the recruits on interpreting the news in harmony with military values and goals. "The true job title for it," David said, "was 'propagandist.'" Donna confirmed this: "They pegged him perfectly. They put him in the b.s. department."

Officers, often with good reason, mistook David's propensity to question orders for smartass backtalk, and David was awarded a steady diet of KP duty. Then he went AWOL for four days in April 1947 to marry Donna. It was a small, church affair, but the families came out, along with the country community, to celebrate the bride and her groom, who, unbeknownst to anyone was, in fact, a fugitive in their midst. Mysteriously, the only punishment was a tongue-lashing doled out by a Sergeant named Hansen, who said with sincere disappointment, "Bamberger, for Chrissake, I thought we was rid of you!"

"You know, I nearly got court-martialed once," David told me.

"Yeah, what for?"

"Well, after I was married, I worked part-time at the golf course near the barracks. I got a dollar an hour, but this is where I made the money. When the course closed, there was David Bamberger with a bag, hunting for lost golf balls."

"You can get court-martialed for collecting golf balls?"

"Well, I'd pick up the ones those officers and other guys couldn't find. I'd clean them up and put them on a tray. Used golf balls, fifty cents. Some major came in there. He was going to buy one but saw his initials on it and said, 'This is mine.' I said, 'Well, bullshit it is!' Let me tell you, he went after me."

KP marked David, and it had nothing to do with the behavioral readjustment program his officers aimed for. "I'd get the order, 'Sift those beans, Bamberger,' and I'm the wise guy replying, 'Why sift them? It's a waste of time.' But no sooner did I begin sifting those hundred-pound sacks of beans than I found that at least 10% of it was stones, and if you cooked the beans as they were, they'd break the GIs' teeth. Food suppliers were selling gravel to the government. That's a symbol. You can have flag waving and send troops over there to Iraq. But you know someone was profiteering by putting gravel in the beans."

David was promoted to the honorable rank of acting corporal, and his incredulous army buddies Ellis, Charley, Chip, and Bernie, rubbed stripes on the dusty '37 Chevy Coupe that he kept on the base, saluting mockingly each time he passed. The promotion was less surprising considering that Major Finley, commanding officer of the Information and Education section, took a shine to his smart-alecky corporal. Aside from preparing news propaganda, David cleverly ran a high-school equivalency program, since most non-commissioned officers lacked high-school diplomas, and diplomas were required for promotion. He coordinated night extension courses since many officers worked days, and he discovered that the equivalency scores could be submitted to any state. Because David quickly discerned that Arkansas had the most charitable standards, dozens of young men from states as disparate as New York, Georgia, and Ohio wound up earning high school certificates from Arkansas, known as "The Natural State," the motto of which is "The people rule."

When David wasn't processing high school equivalency tests or working KP, he took college extension courses so that by the time he was discharged, he was required to attend Kent State for only three years to obtain a business degree. He devised a game with Charley Duffley, a six-foot, redheaded friend, the two trying to stump each other with a new word each day to improve their vocabularies.

At the end of his stretch, the army tried to sign David for the reserves. "I told them, 'No thanks. I've had enough.' I get back home, and the guys I went to high school with said, 'Man, you really screwed up. We go to the meeting, and we don't do nothing but shoot pool and play cards. Once a year, you take a vacation for two weeks and get full pay.' Those guys, every one, got called back to Korea."

Talking to David, Donna, and their friends brought back recollections of the 1950s for me, since they were mostly of my parents' generation, young men and women struggling in those years to make and support families. Suburbs expanded, and large subdivisions were built, particularly in the Southwest. GIs received loans for homes: no down payment, 4% interest. Door-to-door salespeople for makeup, brushes, encyclopedias, flatware, pots, magazines, containers, and vacuum cleaners were ubiquitous. Doors would open to strangers, even if they were then only turned away as an annoyance. The direct sales business invoked the Willy Lomans of the *Death of a Salesman* world, lonesome men and women, usually down on their luck.

I visited the Airharts, Donna and David's close friends from Navarre. Don Airhart was tall and thin, a bit of a Gary Cooper look about him even at nearly eighty, and he seemed to suffer only a slight tremor. His wife Donna was also on the tall side, in great shape, very articulate. The Airharts went into deep rewind, remembering the late 1940s and 1950s when they had started out, all but penniless.

I was astounded by how closely their lives paralleled David and Donna's for almost a decade: both couples started out living with their parents; both had three children—two boys and a girl; they went into the same businesses; and they moved to the same parts of the country.

While living at Crossroads, David commuted first to the Kent State extension in Canton and then for a year and a half to the main campus to finish his courses. Donna gave birth to their first son on February 15,

1949 and named him David. The Airharts' son, born the same year, took the father's name, Don. As graduation approached, David interviewed with both Metropolitan and New York Life Insurance companies, but his heart was set on starting his own business, an automobile dealership.

David had always loved cars and couldn't resist car lots, doubtless connecting them with his father. While visiting a Studebaker showroom and looking over the spaceship-shaped automobiles with their chrome nose cones, he overheard a couple of men trying to sign up the owner with the French company Renault, which had begun producing the 4CV. In those days, next to a Chevy Fleetline or a Mercury Landcruiser, the Renaults looked scarcely more serious than a toy. David picked up the literature extolling the virtues of the 4CV, its low price and gas efficiency—which aroused only hypothetical interest since gas then sold at 19¢ a gallon. The company required the purchase of two cars in order to qualify for a dealership, and David, material in hand, went directly to Don, who ran a small used car lot down by Navarre's railroad tracks. "You and I can go into this and really clean up." Don listened, unfortunately.

The first Renault dealership in the state of Ohio was opened in Navarre. David and Don rented a showroom and a three-bay garage. Don explained, "We had no money. Dave and I would get the Reamer brothers, who owned the property, into a card game. That's how we made the rent." They had sunk every nickel they had, and then some, into their Renault venture, and it wouldn't take long for their initial euphoria to metamorphose into anxiety and then outright despair. Ohioans had no interest in complicating their lives with a peculiar foreign car half the size of anything else on the road and carrying the name of Louis Renault, a Nazi collaborator.

Meanwhile, a couple of traveling salesmen, a bit older, seeing immediately that the Renault dealership was doomed, came by the showroom and flaunted their earnings from peddling Airway vacuum cleaners. Don said, "It looked so good. They'd get a twenty-five dollar commission on each one. They took us out, showed us how it was done: 'If you got a minute, ma'am, there is something we'd like to show ya today.'"

Being a door-to-door vacuum cleaner salesman was anything but glamorous, but what immediately appealed to David was that he could work a hundred hours a week if he so chose. He would be his own boss, following his own instincts. With his gift for sales and his willingness to put in long days, David quickly rose to top salesman for the Akron office, for which he was awarded an expense-paid trip to New Orleans. It was an auspicious trip, as he was introduced to district sales managers from around the country. He was proud of selling twenty-eight vacuum cleaners in a month but soon humbled on discovering that others had sold fifty or more. He sometimes struggled to give even two demonstrations a day. It became readily apparent that sales were easier in other parts of the country.

The Navarre house had been partitioned to create space for both Hes and the young Bamberger family, but Hes took a nursing position in Yakima, Washington, sensing that they all needed even more space. In Navarre, David felt the sting of both veiled and overt family disapproval. His Uncle Voyance, who became director of Fort Wayne Corrugated Box Company in Indiana, scolded Hes and thereby, indirectly, David. "Door-to-door sales is not a respectable job for Davy. He has a college education." Donna's parents and Hes herself harbored similar sentiments, although they may not have expressed them so explicitly. The family's opinions only fomented anger, and then angry determination, on David's part.

When the Ward Stilson Company of Indiana offered David a position as the Cincinnati branch manager for sales of Masonette dresses, he couldn't resist the move away; besides, the job title had an executive ring. He convinced Don once again that they could "clean up," this time in the dress business, and Don was hired to open an office in Nashville, both men leaving their families in Navarre for a spartan, boarding-house existence. Ultimately, their jobs differed little from vacuum cleaner sales; the two canvassed door-to-door in different neighborhoods, recruiting women to sell Masonette dresses to friends and neighbors. Don complained, "The women had a million excuses for not selling their dresses. We were starving to death in the dress business."

After five months, David was ready for a move but not keen on returning to Navarre and his disapproving relatives. Through contacts he'd made in New Orleans, he planned to go to Tucumcari, New Mexico, where business was developing and there was little competition in vacuum cleaner sales. David's brother Tom wound up in Oklahoma, supporting a wife and two kids and putting himself through law school, also selling for Airway. David had connected Tom with the Oklahoma branch manager, and soon afterwards Tom wrote his brother, "Davy, you got to come out here. It's so easy. You go to the door, and they just invite you in."

David found himself roping the baby's bed and a mattress to the roof of the car, packing in his family and what little they had, and leaving Ohio with a solemn promise to Donna that after two years and accumulating savings of $10,000, he would bring her back home and make a comfortable life. It was a promise he wouldn't keep. The young Bamberger family left on Thanksgiving and drove as far as Claremore, Oklahoma, before getting caught in a freak snowstorm that forced them to rent a hotel room on their last dollar. When they arrived in Norman, they didn't have a dime left and ended up in an old, converted Navy barracks on the south side of the University of Oklahoma campus. The quarters had high ceilings and a wood stove, so that residents had to go out in the brisk winter air and chop wood—nothing new to the Bambergers, given their earlier days at Crossroads. David, Donna, and the baby moved in, squatters posing as a graduate student family.

Still imagining that he'd end up in New Mexico, David was forced to work for the Oklahoma City Airway office. That first month and every month after, he was its top salesman. David told me that in order to be a good salesman, whether of ephemeral widgets or of public policies such as environmental restoration, you first have to be sold on your own product. He explained that he genuinely liked Airway vacuum cleaners. They sat like a fireplug, and the hose hooked to a swivel so that you could even jump rope with it if you wanted. You could put a rubber ring on the floor and put the hose to it; the machine sucked so hard you couldn't pull it loose. There was an attachment with naphthalene crystals for de-mothing closets, or you could mix triethylene glycol—used to deice car fuel lines—with camphor and scent a room.

David also explained the power of initiative and the pressure a salesman could apply once allowed into a home. "People give up their liberty. They can't make love or go put together a sandwich, and you can be damn convincing. You can embarrass the hell out of them, vacuum their bed, and say, 'Look, this is your skin! You spend a third of your life here, and you leave behind two and a half pounds of your skin each year.'"

Since business was so good, the Airharts moved out to Oklahoma City as well, and the families bought houses in a subdivision called The Village. Like other veterans, the men applied for GI loans for financing. Subdivisions were booming in the area, and it didn't take long before David was tracking down home buyers and making Airway sales before the last nail had been hammered into their new places.

Despite his devotion to the Airway products, David switched to Kirby, a machine he never cared for. David admitted feeling like a prostitute when he sold Kirbys, but the Airway Company at the time didn't provide an opportunity for him to advance toward his own distributorship, and once Airway's managers did move into a distribution system similar to Kirby's, they made the mistake of selling machines on credit. This policy would lead, in part, to the company's collapse. Kirby manufacturers demanded payment for the machines; the individual distributorships were responsible for customer credit.

David was recruited to be a Kirby sales manager in Tyler, Texas, and he shifted from peddling machines directly to organizing and motivating a sales force. Don was made a field counselor in nearby Longview, and it would be the last move that he and David would make together, both selling their homes in Oklahoma City and buying new ones in Texas. Within a year, David suffered his first significant betrayal in business. The regional manager swindled him on commissions, and in a fury, David quit Kirby. Donna was pregnant with their second child and, without a clear future, returned to her family in Ohio. David came down with walking pneumonia and was left to ponder his next move.

When David recalls the low periods, I try to imagine myself in his place: what it must be like to have the responsibility of a young family, to spend so much time on the road, crammed in cheap hotel rooms with other salesmen sleeping on the floor, intruding on strangers in their homes, and having only transient friendships. Even in a recent conversation, David said to me, "I have countless acquaintances but few close friends." He possessed a singular determination, sometimes anger-driven, that propelled him through adversity or gave him the strength to follow his convictions against strong opposition in business or on environmental issues. I'm often reminded of how the ranch house on Selah is set between two of the more melancholy sounding tracts: High Lonesome and Windsong. Windsong was named after the music fencing wire made when a strong wind came down the slope. David said to me, "That fence will actually sing to you."

Adversity, however, was the turning point that brought David to San Antonio. The Kirby supervisor in the Dallas office called David, having heard that he had quit, and offered him the chance to buy into a distributorship in either Waco or San Antonio. Fortunately he had saved money just as he vowed he would, and after visiting the library and studying Chamber of Commerce materials, he couldn't resist the sales potential of San Antonio's growing population and its four airbases. Attaining the franchise consisted primarily of buying out the previous distributor's inventory, which amounted to $3,000. While Donna was still in Ohio, he packed the car and set up operations with a new cast of characters—Bert, Otis, Red, Maria, Fay, and no small number of others.

David told me, "I always wanted to make money and become rich because I was afraid to be poor. I wanted to be able to take care of my wife and my kids. And I would never use credit. I paid cash for everything. And I still do. I have this ethic that you don't need to be spending and buying every damned thing that comes along."

It's hard not to applaud David's conviction about not wasting money, which can be extrapolated to his deep aversion to any kind of waste, particularly the exploitation and destruction of the environment by the endless production of unnecessary goods and the trappings of excess. In those years while David practiced his own brand of asceticism, he was igniting the entrepreneurial spirit in his new sales team, exhorting them to work with the same rigor as himself. He read that carrot juice could reverse the effects of alcoholism and decided to serve it at his Monday morning sales meetings, blessing it as the elixir of success. No angle would be left untried. He learned for the first time that he had peculiar power over people. Maria, a Russian woman, became so eager to sell Kirbys during the Monday pep-talks that she couldn't be held in her chair. She went on to become a national sales champion. In fact, David's organization achieved Kirby's national title, winning two Plymouth Valiants.

Meanwhile, Donna remembers Saturday nights in San Antonio, loading the car up with three kids by then. Instead of to a film or a restaurant, David would drive them to various, often grim neighborhoods, his family sitting in the car while he collected on unpaid notes or repossessed Kirbys when households couldn't make the payments.

The Airharts might once more have followed in David's footsteps and become wealthy in San Antonio, but Don's wife had had enough of living like a nomad; she had little interest in city life and wanted desperately, like David's Donna, to return home to Ohio. Donna Airhart would shortly get her wish, and back in Navarre Don returned to used car sales and added a car rental business as well. Donna trained as a hairdresser and then opened a beauty parlor where she worked until their kids graduated from college.

Hester returned to her home in Navarre. In front of the town post office, in her usual cloud of thoughts, she stepped into the street crossing without looking and was hit by a car. Unlike the three Bamberger men whose lives were halted by, respectively, a train, a crane, and a plane, Hester survived the blow of the car fender, but not without a long convalescence followed by arthritis so severe she couldn't climb her back steps or hoist herself from a tub that held her captive in cooling water. The doctors prescribed cortisone; instead, she took her medical treatment into her own hands. A book by Dan Dale Alexander called *Arthritis*

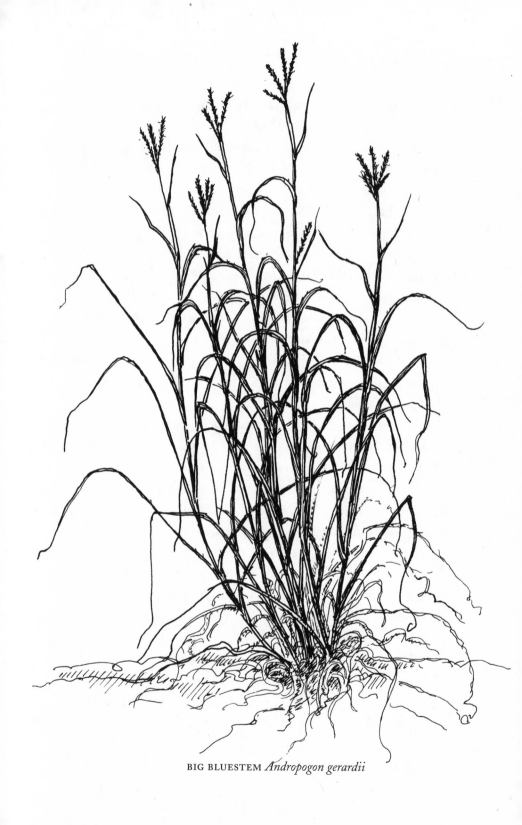

BIG BLUESTEM *Andropogon gerardii*

and Common Sense had just been released and was destined, in a revised edition, to become a number-one best seller in 1956. Dr. Alexander, who had witnessed his mother's suffering and purposely induced arthritis in himself, devised a strict daily diet which included an inordinate amount of cod liver oil. Hester saw a specialist who said, "Mrs. Bamberger, you are a nurse, a woman of science. Do you really think all that cod liver oil will lubricate your joints?" He still ended up prescribing a diet that hardly differed from Dr. Alexander's.

The family, David in particular, was astounded when Hester cured herself completely. They were equally amazed at her fanaticism for all-natural foods, her refrigerator stocked with packets of herbs and plants. Her gardens became ever more important in her life, though it wasn't unusual for her to lose track of what she had planted and where. Her garden was strictly devoid of artificial chemicals.

Donna Airhart recalled Hes coming to her beauty parlor on the hottest summer day. "We were busy, women suffering a long wait in heat. Hes said, 'It's okay. I'll wait outside.'" Without the slightest stiffness in her shoulders or arms, she lifted off her blouse and sat in the shade of a tree. Donna said, "She was a naturalist, all right."

Carter Tank

CARTER TANK, on the higher east-facing slopes, looks clearly human-made, with Blue Ridge Road crossing the top of a steep earthen dam. It may not be the most magical of Selah's bodies of water, but it has its particular mystique. Only months earlier, just after New Year's, the whole area was enveloped in freezing mist, and I had startled three deer at the water's edge. They ran in a kind of evasive glide up the steep hillside, and the high ground under them and the stripped winter trees looked more imaginary than solid.

Carter Tank belongs to the original portion of the preserve, the first purchase of just over 3,000 acres. The tank bears the last owner's name. The section forms the eastern watershed that extends two miles from Carter Tank to Round Mountain and includes The Center, Madrone Lake, and the ranch house. In these hills, the layers of Cretaceous limestone show through the vegetation on the slopes, recording in legible striations the comings and goings of an ancient sea. This was the part of the ranch that required the most rigorous restoration, the part David refers to when interviewed by the press or giving talks to tour groups, claiming that he was inspired by Bromfield to buy the poorest, most badly overgrazed piece of land and restore it. Soon after the Carter purchase, he bought from Alice Sergeant four hundred acres in the northeast that afforded a little more watershed around Miller Creek. The last major acquisition came from the neighboring Heath family. It comprised the western 2,043 acres, including the tallest point on the preserve, with its fossil beds and dinosaur tracks. It also includes the lower northwest pastureland, "Little Mexico," and "The Sahara," for endangered species.

David's interest in real estate followed a progression that coincided with his ascent in the business world, and it was his passion for both owning property and sharing it that would lead to his becoming an environmental activist. That process started in the early 1970s and reached a peak in the late 1980s and mid-1990s with Ann Richards in the governor's office, Lady Bird Johnson advocating Texas park development, and President Clinton showing sensitivity to environmental concerns by insisting that "A healthy economy and a healthy environment are not at odds with each other; they are essential to each other."

With the success of his Kirby office in the 1950s, David could start considering investment opportunities. He no longer worked direct door-to-door sales but instead took over hiring, management, and collection on defaulted accounts—hardnosed, thankless work. The Korean War was on, and San Antonio's air bases revved into action with training and large movements of personnel and materials. David learned that he could acquire houses that had been mortgaged through GI loans, which could be assumed. A trade had developed in buying and selling GI equities. GIs purchased homes with no money down, and after one or two years merely the interest would be covered. Some military personnel being shipped out were looking for ways to unload their payments. After coming across such a GI, one who was in debt and willing to turn over payments, David worked out the transaction through his friend and attorney Guy Bonham, who said that there had to be some financial consideration. "Well, what about a dollar?" David responded. With one dollar and a $12.50 title-processing fee, David entered the real estate business. By a combination of ongoing inflation and weekends spent painting shutters and manicuring yards, he transformed unwanted GI properties into profitable real estate. He obtained a broker's license, acquired additional houses, and rented them to cover loans. He soon graduated to purchasing commercial office property and an apartment house. After the unsettled life of door-to-door sales in Ohio, Oklahoma, and Texas, a career his family held in rather low esteem, David saw real estate as an avenue to security, a way to consolidate and build on hard-won earnings. Unlike stocks, real estate was something tangible. His rebellion against his family in the north was finally paying dividends in the south.

David's rebellious spirit would lead him time and again into controversy—in the social arena, in business, and even in the environmental community. In an act motivated more by a wish to finesse prevailing stupidity and aid a friend than as an overt initiative for desegregation, he facilitated the purchase of a home for one of his employees, Fay Williams, an impeccably dressed black man who would close his Kirby sales with a prayer. "Every time Fay wanted to look at a home," David explained to me, "the realtors would see a black man and scoot back into their cars. They wouldn't even talk to him. Fay described to me a house that interested him in north San Antonio, but what could he do? He couldn't even see it. He gave me the name of the realtor, and I called for an appointment, pretending that I was moving to the city. I brought a couple of Kirby salesmen with me, telling them to unlock the windows while I talked in the kitchen. That night, Fay and his wife Gladys saw the house and wanted it. The following day I called the realtor, saying that I would not wait for my wife. I'd just take it. I didn't argue the price. I told Guy what I was trying to do. That's attorney-client privilege, and he wrote in a clause where the land could be 'assigned,' not unusual at the time. The seller signed the contract. I then assigned it to Fay Williams. By that time, it was too late to do anything, and all hell broke loose. The neighborhood organized and threatened us on the phone every half-hour, twenty-four hours a day, warning us to watch our kids. Donna was hysterical, and I don't mind telling you I was frightened myself. But the other part of the story is that Fay and Gladys were such outstanding people that they were having yard parties for their neighbors within a year."

In 1959, David turned over a portion of his San Antonio real estate holdings and bought his first ranch, 205 acres in Bulverde, a small German community then, with Speck's country store at its center, only thirty minutes north of San Antonio off Route 281. They dubbed it the "Cinco B" after the five Bambergers. Donna and the three kids remember it nostalgically, a country escape from their home in a development, a dimension in their lives that most other people didn't have. The boys matured into men, learned to ride and shoot, gained a sense of responsibility, and worked for spending money while developing respect for the land. They cooled their first beers hidden in a wooden water tank common on old-time ranches. Deena, not unlike her father in his youth, kept a pony of her own that she adored.

While it might not have been apparent at the time or even for some while afterwards, the purchase of the Bulverde ranch was a major step in David's growth as an environmentalist. For the first time, he had his own country fiefdom, a small one by Texas standards, but immense when compared to his childhood home at Crossroads. He understood Bromfield's description of the farmer: "the happiest of men for he inhabits a world full of wonder and excitement over which he rules as a small god." As so many of Selah's workshop participants would do later, David enrolled in courses on ranching, conservation, and the agricultural legacy of the Hill Country. At his Methodist Sunday Bible classes, he befriended Bill McReynolds, a well-known broadcaster and agricultural guru, who in turn introduced him to other ranch and nature experts. David could witness and experience in tangible ways Bromfield's concerns for land damaged by exploitation for a single cash crop—in this case, cotton. In addition, he saw the need to nurture a respect for local farmers with a long regional heritage, much as Hes and Bromfield did the Amish. He could foresee real estate investment potential and the consequent threat of dividing land, erecting fences, and creating "ranchettes" and tract home developments, as San Antonio would inevitably sprawl northward into the fragile Hill Country.

Above all, the Bulverde ranch became a testing ground for what David would accomplish on a far grander scale at Selah. He learned that the overgrowth of Ashe juniper in the wake of overgrazing was a prime culprit in the demise of Hill Country watersheds. Clearing Ashe junipers was the first step in David's version of "land restoration," first on Bulverde and then Selah. As soon as he cleared vast tracts of the juniper and allowed native grasses to return, he could see rapid improvement in land quality. He kept horses and twenty-five mother cows that managed to find their way out at night. David recalled, "I can't tell you how many times the sheriff called after midnight. 'Your cows are out here, Bamberger. They're on the county road.' I'd get up at one or two in the morning and try to round up the damn cows. The right kinds of fences eliminated those hassles."

Bulverde, with its farmed-out cotton field, belonged to Willie Stahl, a rare reincarnation of the original German settlers who had typified the Hill Country. Stahl had worked the land the old-fashioned way, with plow and mule-team, and his body showed it: his broad shoulders stooped, his fingers thickened, and his joints swollen from the grueling work. A competing bid, somewhat higher than the price quoted to David, had been offered for Stahl's land. The competitor, after asking the field's length—which Stahl knew all too well, having tread its 2,800 feet for decades while plowing, seeding, and picking cotton—revealed that it would serve perfectly for an airstrip he had in mind. Locals were already sensitized to the way in which their family lands were being absorbed and they themselves displaced. Willie accepted David's lower offer instead, out of reverence for the land, and in turn David left him the keys, saying, "You keep these." The old farmer was dumbstruck, as were other locals when they heard that Stahl could come and go on his former land. Almost forty years after the Bulverde purchase, in the first issue of a local tabloid, *Heartland Voices,* David wrote about Willie's value to the Bambergers: "He stayed connected. It just made sense in many ways to listen to what a person like Mr. Stahl had to teach you about the land that he has lived on and worked all his life." David said it more bluntly to me. "The land isn't worth shit if you don't share it." Perhaps Willie Stahl invoked ancestral imprints of David's own Swiss-German agrarian values—grittiness, hard work, a deep reverence for the earth. They paralleled much of the rural spirit of his childhood.

Willie Stahl was far from being the only guest at the "Cinco B." Donna hosted Girl Scout troops at Bulverde, the three kids invited their adolescent friends, and David would bring almost anyone home to dinner, whether a vacuum cleaner salesman or a farmer. Hes' welcoming spirit was ingrained in him. Understandably, though, the parade of unexpected guests that the irrepressibly hail-fellow-well-met David produced at the dinner table became a chronic annoyance for Donna.

In the 1960s, David became, as he had vowed to do, a wealthy man. By 1969 he was wildly successful at Church's Fried Chicken, which he invested in purely out of an alignment of planetary forces better known as dumb luck. It became a company that he and Bill Church synergistically expanded with uncanny, sometimes wacky vision and solid industriousness. While David was proud of his financial accomplishments, the trappings of wealth—the ability to purchase luxury cars, join country clubs, mix familiarly with the affluent social ranks, and travel first class—repulsed him. He did, however, purchase property on the shore of Lake Travis with a double boat dock that floated on Styrofoam. There, he had a 17-foot powerboat to take the kids (by then in their teens), friends, and business associates water skiing. The country music star Willie Nelson bought a nearby bankrupt country club, and music carried over the water from Nelson's all-night bashes.

When David described the Lake Travis property, I sensed strong but mixed feelings. He recalled special times and fun shared with the family; on the other hand, supplying food and alcohol for a crowd each weekend and maintaining the boat, which he kept immaculate, soon lost their charm. No matter how much Donna urged David to scale back at work and learn to relax, he was constitutionally incapable of repose.

David may have been attentive to operations and expansion of Church's, but his passion and sense of comfort came from ranch-land ownership. He purchased 505 acres with a mile of Guadalupe River frontage only ten miles north of Bulverde. The land was undeveloped countryside with the exception of a house with no power or running water, rumored to be the oldest in Kendall County. The property was situated only forty minutes out of San Antonio and an hour and a half from Austin.

The Guadalupe is one of the most beautiful and historical rivers in Texas, first explored in 1689 by Alonzo de León, the Spaniard who christened it. It emerges from springs just west of Fredericksburg, crosses part of the Edwards Plateau through the Balcones Escarpment, and descends to the Gulf plains, meandering through Victoria and emptying into San Antonio Bay. Primitive artifacts reveal that the banks of the Guadalupe have been inhabited for thousands of years and several tribes lived there when Europeans arrived. The Spanish built missions in Victoria and San Marcos, and these were followed by settlements of Irish and Germans, with Texas towns and counties coming to bear their names—Kerrville, New Braunfels, and McCulloch. Texas lore likes to claim that on October 2, 1835, the first shots for Texas independence were fired in Gonzales on the Guadalupe, even though precedents of violent confrontations between Mexican officials and Texas settlers began as early as 1826 with the Fredonian Rebellion.

In the early 1970s, a different sort of rebellion occurred in the effort to liberate the banks of the Guadalupe River for public recreation, and David's affiliation with this movement marked his debut in environmental activism. According to *Texas Environmental Profiles,* Texas is the second largest state, with the second largest population in America, and yet 94.3 percent of the land is privately owned. The lack of public lands is paradoxically the result of the "Texas War of Independence" and the decision by nineteen-century Texas leaders to sell landholdings to pay off the war debt and to encourage settlers to develop and solidify the new state. To this day, private land rights in Texas are sacred and fiercely defended.

While David fell in love with land ownership, he also had a deep conviction that natural resources belonged to everyone. The Guadalupe River was a canoeist's dream, with its limpid spring waters, rapids, limestone bluffs, towering bald cypresses, oaks, and open grasslands. Private land owners were vehemently against camping or trespassing because of littering and property damage, not to mention the intrusion on privacy. The problem of littering was particularly severe where state roads wound across the river, creating abused points of access. Some private land-owners erected fences and even threatened canoeists, reportedly punctur-ing their hulls with .22-caliber perforations. In response, a small group of canoeists began citing the National Wild and Scenic Rivers Act, which stipulates the public right to appreciate, protect, and use recreationally designated river frontage. Even though the Guadalupe was not one of the rivers listed in the National Act, they began lobbying the Texas state legislature for recreational access.

To the serious displeasure of his neighbors, David put up signs along the river's edge on his property, saying "Canoeists Welcome." The "big shot" from the fried chicken business further embittered his neighbors when he suggested that area landowners sell waterfront property to the state with the stipulation that it become parkland. Neighbors conjured up dreaded images of hippies arriving from all corners of the state, pitching their tents, and leaving a trail of trash and damage.

David went in person to the Texas Parks and Wildlife Department with two ideas. First he advocated the creation of parks at river crossings. He argued that the state should exercise eminent domain and purchase an acre of land at each corner of the bridges crossing the Guadalupe to create mini-parks. The state could provide picnic tables and proper gar-bage disposal, and the public could enjoy a great Texas natural resource, as was their right. Instead of roadside parks, there would be riverside parks. As meritorious as this idea was, it received no consideration. On a second visit, David inquired about the possibility of creating a state park, and the official said, "We'd like to have a park on the Guadalupe River. It's needed, but we've never been able to purchase any land there—the people are against it."

"Well, I have an ideal spot." David responded. "I have 505 acres of pristine land on the north side of the river. I want it to become a state park."

"But what are you asking for it?" The official was expecting an outra-geous price for the ever more valuable land with development sprawling north from San Antonio.

"You can set the price. People have the right to enjoy the river."

The department called in surveyors from West Texas. They had to go through four private gates on an old county dirt road to get back to the land. David took a bulldozer down to build an entrance and cut a road to the river. Though the land was carefully assessed, two years passed before the department acted, setting up a commission. David assumed that establishing a park would be easy and was taken off guard when landowners rose up vehemently against the project, appearing at meetings to voice their disapproval, often intimidating the politically appointed commissioners.

With a group of Sierra Club friends, David began attending meetings where decisions were postponed time and again. In the end, hundreds of pro-park advocates packed the commission and overwhelmed the landowners. The leading commissioner sent a note to David requesting another postponement and David, incensed, wrote back, "No, this is your last chance." David recalled that six commissioners deliberated over his response and ultimately decided in favor of establishing a park. Editorials in local papers at the time said that despite the current fury, local land-owners would ultimately be thankful for the park in years to come.

David's piece of land became the cornerstone of the now 1,938-acre Guadalupe River State Park, established in 1981. In 1985, the Nature Conservancy acquired an adjacent 2,293 acres, which became known as the Honey Creek Preserve. The conservancy subsequently sold the area to the Texas Parks and Wildlife Department, who made it into a unit of the Guadalupe River State Park. It was turned into the limited-access Honey Creek State Natural Area, featuring interpretive guided tours of flora, fauna, and geology.

I had unintentionally blundered into the park areas while search-ing out a pet groomer for my two Maltese dogs, whose fur had become embedded with burrs, twigs, and seeds. I crossed the Guadalupe River six times looking for the turnoff that would bring me to a groomer whose business bordered on a wooded tract north of Canyon Lake. The driveway passed through fenced areas that resembled training facilities for miniature horses, and a middle-aged blond woman in short cutoffs sat smoking at the doorstep when I pulled up. My small white dogs danced and barked impetuously around her gentlemanly German shepherd. I soon learned that besides boarding and grooming, dog training was a major part of the operation, in particular for bomb-sniffing dogs for international sale. The woman complained that her husband hid semtex in the workroom without telling her. "It's not really dangerous," she conceded, "but I'd still like to know where it is." Apparently, the husband also had a DEA license and took their mild- mannered German shepherd on San Antonio public school visits, busting kids with drugs and weapons. "You should see the stupid looks on their faces." My dogs came out impeccably clipped and wearing black and orange scarves as if it were Halloween in April, both at less than the cost of one clipping at a *toilettage* in Paris.

Driving back to Johnson City, I could see the pattern David followed as he purchased land farther north, deeper into the Hill Country, while remaining only an hour's drive from his business offices in San Antonio. In the larger picture, the Guadalupe River property, though more than twice the size of his Bulverde ranch, was just a sideshow since he never used it beyond its investment value. As you head north, the hills and canyons become more pronounced; properties appear much more extensive; and small towns like Blanco, Round Mountain, and Johnson City retain something of their original Hill Country character, with historic courthouses, jails, stark white churches, country stores, banks, auction barns, grist and cotton mills, dance halls, saloons, cemeteries, and original homesteads. Towns like Twin Sisters, Payton, and Albert have all but evaporated after droughts, bankruptcies, and crop and industry failures. There is even a town called Blowout just fifteen miles northwest of Johnson City. It was named after a nearby cave where hundreds of thousands of bats deposited large quantities of guano. The resulting admixture of ammonia and other gases produced a massive explosion upon being detonated by a lightning strike at the cave's mouth. What is clear even today on a drive back from the Guadalupe River is that land was cheap because no one could run a profitable ranch where the proliferation of Ashe juniper and erosion followed in the wake of overgrazing by goats and mohair sheep. Like the steel industry in the northeast, the cotton and mohair industries in Texas were hurt by foreign competition as well as by development of synthetic materials.

Almost every press clipping or article on the Bamberger Ranch Preserve quotes David's desire to purchase the worst possible piece of land with the intent of restoring it using a blend of Bromfield's methods and ideas of his own. Having traveled throughout the state of Texas for almost twenty years and seen the potential for rapid development, he could easily predict that land only fifty miles from both Austin and San Antonio would someday turn around in value, particularly if restored to a healthy natural state and enriched with creeks and ponds. Stockbrokers, lawyers, doctors, and professionals of all sorts would want their own ranch, ranchette, or piece of rural property to escape the city grind. Texas ranches would become status symbols.

In May 1969, just two weeks after Church's Fried Chicken went public, David purchased an isolated tract of 3,020 acres near Johnson City. It was known as the Carter Ranch, although Carter himself had lost the land. It had been put up for action and purchased by Carter's business partner from Beaumont, who in turn sold it to David. Carter and his son, both lawyers, showed up at David's San Antonio office demanding that David sell the property back to them, claiming that a previous agreement had been violated, one in which Carter would purchase the ranch back from his partner. After refusing, David was hit with a lawsuit and once again consulted his attorney, who remarked, "You are always bringing me something a little different. They can sue, but you will prevail. Verbal agreements for the sale of real estate are not valid in the state of Texas no matter how many witnesses there may be."

Ultimately, David had to win the worst property in Blanco County, not just once but twice. It had one functional well that produced "gyp" water the color of "a bloody Mary," as he would report in a *New Yorker* profile two decades later. The ranch house—bearing little resemblance to what it is now, with its extensions, glassed-in gallery, and display cases

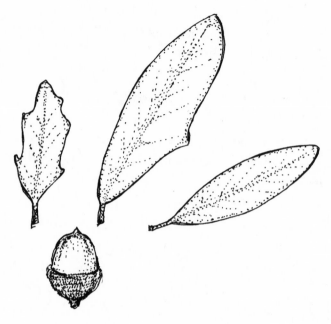

PLATEAU LIVE OAK *Quercus fusiformis*

full of Indian arrow points, birds' nests, and fossils—had been used previously for serious drinking and hell-raising, the hunting so poor on the cedar-choked land that the only good targets were the house's thoroughly pitted bedroom ceilings.

Much of the environmental literature concerning the Hill Country discusses the threat of land development, the worst of which was being instigated by speculators in the early 1970s. Steeped in the real estate business, David became alarmed by Blanco County's vulnerability to land speculation and organized a public campaign to keep it in check. Because clear land registration controls had not been established as they had in neighboring counties, "exploiters," as he labeled them, could buy large tracts and subdivide them without registering them individually. Therefore, these people could pay taxes at the far lower rate for an undeveloped ranch, as opposed to residential lots, and at the same time take advantage of local government resources.

David once again hired his own attorney to research Texas laws to determine who can impose controls on subdivisions outside cities. Texas had relevant legal provisions under the mandate of the Texas Water Quality Board, particularly with respect to Blanco's proximity to the Pedernales River area, and also under civil statutes giving land-control power to county commissioners. David brashly confronted Blanco county officials, including Mike Barrow, county judge at the time, explaining in an article for the *Blanco County News* how land exploiters operate almost like funeral directors selling coffins with music:

> They take the guy from the city pressures, give him pretty music with a hard sell pitch, bring him out to the beauty of the Hill Country and sell him a piece of land for $50 down and $50 a month. The cheap taxes and clean air of Blanco County are not hard to sell so the guy purchases his piece of land not thinking about a road or a well for water or a source of electricity. . . . When all the tracts are sold the developer disappears and these landowners become voters that can put a commissioner out of office if he does not promise to furnish better roads, water, and sewage improvements and so on.

David handed Judge Barrow copies of legal statutes, along with accounts of precedent-setting actions in Kendall County, insisting, "You must take the initiative."

David followed up the hearing by writing a petition to the same officials, and he began a drive, including placing a full-page ad in *The Blanco County News* to collect supportive signatures. He began his advertisement with a fly-over scenario portraying a villainous dialog between a scheming land speculator and his lawyer, saying essentially that beautiful Blanco County was ripe for the taking. David saw himself in the role of Paul Revere: "The speculators are coming!"

Pioneers of Franchising

IN THE EARLY 1960s, David's crews for Kirby consisted of tough-luck salesmen, summer students, and part-timers in a business that reeked of rejection. "The turnover was 200%, and I'd lose someone every week," David said. "So I created the 'add-a-man program.' Let's say you sold five machines. I'd take you to a local store named O.P.O. (One Price Only) where you had a choice of hundreds of suits for $39.95 and I'd buy you one. If you sold another five, I'd buy you a pair of Florsheims, the best shoes in those days. For other sales, you'd get a tie or shirt. You'd make a better impression on your sales calls and of course save money. And if you brought in a new salesman, you'd get a reward. Well, someone brought in a smart, good-looking guy in his thirties, light hair and friendly smile. His name was George W. (Bill) Church Jr."

Bill Church had been a country club golf pro but couldn't make ends meet, so he joined David's distributorship selling Kirby sweepers. He and David quickly formed a friendship. However, under pressure from his family, Bill left Kirby to direct operations of the restaurant business created by his father, George W. Church Sr., who had died in 1956. After spending more than twenty years in the poultry business selling incubators, George Church had started a small store, Church's Fried Chicken to Go, near the Alamo in San Antonio. At the time the fast-food industry had barely developed beyond the traditional hotdog and ice cream stands that had been around even before World War II. McDonald's was just a locally successful hamburger joint run by two brothers in California until the entrepreneur Ray Croc, impressed with the restaurant's popularity, exceptionally low prices, and friendly name, entered into a franchising agreement. Church's concept was to sell inexpensive, fresh-tasting fried chicken in quantity from low-overhead, take-out venues. Church believed that society was rapidly changing; Americans were grabbing quick meals, for instance, and becoming ever more dependent on cars. He understood that take-out food would be popular in a mobile society. One of the keys to a unique product was the old man's secret marinade. It became legendary, second only to the eleven mysterious herbs and spices Colonel Sanders used when he came out of retirement to start Kentucky Fried Chicken. David has always acknowledged Church Sr. as "America's fast-food prophet."

Church Sr. began opening more stores in San Antonio, with a central distribution point for chicken, flour, marinade ingredients, and cooking fat. Chicken was the only product Church sold until in 1955 he added jalapeño peppers and French fries. Although family members ran almost the entire operation, which had grown to four stores by the time Church died, it was barely profitable. The family held a meeting and asked Bill to assume operational responsibility. Bill was granted the power to do what he thought was necessary to make the business viable, and he began seeking investors to support product research and restaurant expansion.

From the start, Bill Church was both clever and ambitious. He studied all aspects of the business, focusing first on the quality of the product, knowing that as shortening gets older, the flavor of fried food deteriorates. He reasoned that he would have to construct a system to filter out impurities continuously without losing heat while the fryers were in use. Despite having worked with engines and hydraulics in the Navy, he was stumped until the answer came to him from a most unlikely source. He regularly shot the breeze at David's Kirby office, where several of the salesmen—especially Otis, middle-aged and jocular—had become David's accomplices in minor mischief, card games, and sales ideas. Overweight and a drinker, Otis said that he and his wife, both smokers, would simply cough at each other for morning conversation. David told me, "Otis had a thousand ideas each month. Almost all of them weren't worth a damn. But then he'd have one or two that were ingenious. Otis had been in the office listening to Bill talk about designing a filter. He asked, 'Didn't you get any trade-in Electrolux sweepers? Well, just build the thing like an Electrolux. You have a tube and filter and put your pump on the other side.'"

It was a peculiar revelation, the vacuum cleaner and fried chicken worlds happily colliding. Bill went to the metal shop, manufactured a thick steel tube, and placed a bag in it, as in the Electrolux, but one made of steel mesh so fine that it was opaque, although you could blow through it. He bought a hydraulic pump, which he attached to the back of the tube. Pipes were hooked up to the fryer so that the hot shortening with batter and impurities would drop into the tube and be filtered before being circulating back into the vat. Bill also learned the chemistry-text-book lesson that diatomaceous earth—silicon dioxide that comes from fossilized microscopic sea creatures—could be added to the shortening to remove additional impurities.

The pumping system worked brilliantly, but the shortening tasted worse than before, with the tang of bitter pennies. A Kansas-based chemist from Kraft, Church's shortening supplier, came to analyze the system. He explained that the oil had three prime enemies: air, water, and certain metals. In this case, the culprit was a copper pipe that Bill had installed on the return line. Once the pipe was replaced with steel and the new fryer was put into action, sales began to rise within a month, and costs decreased. There was no mystery: the chicken remained fresh-tasting longer, and the shortening didn't need replacing nearly so often. The innovation was a revolution.

David had already achieved what he considered a wonderful life, though his family may at times have thought otherwise. He had built a new home in San Antonio and acquired the Bulverde ranch, his investments and real estate ventures were lucrative, Kirbys were selling well, and he and Donna had good friends. On the down side, it's not surprising, given David's kind of drive, that he wasn't around enough to look after the educational and emotional needs of his kids, a lapse that he now openly regrets. He even feels that his personality—critical nature, determination, ambition—was overwhelming, with decision-making rarely deferred. Donna assumed the role of nurturer, as Hes had in David's childhood, while he emulated, perhaps unintentionally, his own absent father.

David said of those days, "I was always buying something and trying to make it worth more to someone else." However, his investment in Church's Fried Chicken was hardly based on his best business instincts. In fact, he made loans that he doubted would ever be repaid.

David had finished a Monday morning sales meeting, and his re-inspired sweeper sales force had set off for the housing developments of south-central Texas, when Bill Church showed up at the office. He explained that the filter was working and showed a positive sales sheet, but said he needed help to make the payroll and asked for a $1,000 loan. David remembered thinking, "The first damn thing they taught me when I went to the university and took accounting is that if you don't bring in enough money to make the payroll, well, you won't have a decent business." Bill said that he had been spending money on research and development, which left David thinking, incredulously, that Bill was trying to sound like General Motors. In fact, fitting all the fryers with filters, testing the interaction of different flours and shortenings, and reorienting the stores for increased efficiency in cooking and sales had run up costs. Bill promised to repay the loan in a month.

Bill reappeared a month later. David thought, briefly, that he would see his money again, but Bill needed another $1,000. Sales continued strong, but Bill still had outstanding debts. David, now wary, said that he needed some kind of collateral, and Bill proposed interest on the loan, with a thousand shares in the company as a kicker, along with another promise of repayment in a month. David asked for ten hundred-share certificates. David's plan was to give one to the Kirby man who sold the first vacuum cleaner each week, but that scheme never materialized. After waiting several weeks, an annoyed David drove to South San Antonio to ask Bill's sister Virginia, who managed the business office, when he could expect the certificates. Her answer was that Church's couldn't afford the 50¢ forms needed to issue them.

At about this time, David read *The Franchising Boom* by Harry Kursh, a futurist who predicted that franchising would sweep across America.

This sounds, in retrospect, like understatement, since franchising has produced the commercial landscape that we now know so well: fast food, banks, hotels, real estate, pharmacies, and retail outlets. It's a landscape so homogeneous that every highway exit from Maine to San Diego looks cloned. I had a post-Kurshian epiphany one night in West Virginia. While I waited for take-out at an Applebee's, a lanky twenty-six-year-old in formal white shirt and tie, just off work, struck up a monologue on his having earned $80,000 a year as a mortician, and he had already organized partners to begin franchising his funereal expertise. I had an unnerving vision of all of us processed, from birth to death, through an unbroken chain of age-appropriate franchises.

Harry Kursh outlined principles and advantages of franchising that seem obvious now: signage and architectural imagery as instantly recognizable in the Dakota badlands as in Times Square; a single advertising and marketing message broadcastable anywhere at all; bulk inventory purchasing in huge volume at reduced prices, logo on every item; frugal exploitation of futures markets; minimum consideration of easily replaceable personnel. The entrepreneurial litany goes on and on. David realized that the Kurshian paradigm was what Bill Church had going and that Church Sr. had started a kind of business that was far ahead of his time.

With business improving but still without capital, Bill proposed that David buy properties and lease them to Church's for twenty years, with the company covering property taxes and expenses, receiving a percentage of sales for his trouble. Tom Bamberger remembers an annual poker game in San Antonio where Bill described his father's enterprise, explaining that it wasn't even a restaurant. David then told Tom, "I'm thinking of buying into this business."

"Hell, let's go check it out."

They drove down to the store, no more than a cement-block construction at the back of a parking lot with boxes stacked around it. A sign on a homely brown background near the flat roof read "Fried Chicken 49¢" in muddied yellow. The employees were young Mexican Americans. Tom said to David, "What the hell is this? You get two pieces of chicken for 49¢, and you're losing money every time you sell it."

David said, "Wait a minute. You have to try some."

Tom did, and he admitted that the chicken was terrific, having been marinated and freshly cooked. Still, he was convinced that they couldn't make money selling two pieces at 49¢. David said, "Well, that could all change."

By 1962, Church's had expanded to eight stores in the San Antonio area. Bill Church had greater ambitions and at the same time was somewhat disgruntled with his position in the family business since he was putting in the hundred-hour weeks and the innovations while his relatives, some not even living in San Antonio, were profiting. Bill met David to present yet another proposition: to create an entirely new company, separate from Church's Fried Chicken, called Church's Food Service Industry. He wanted David to be president. Bill negotiated with his family, offering to manage the stores and operations in San Antonio for them while starting the separate venture. David's contribution was critical: he would put up $55,000. Others put in smaller amounts. Bill contributed his knowledge, imagination, and hard work.

Years later, the company accountant would ask, "Bill, how did Bamberger get all these shares?"

Bill looked at him incredulously: "You're the financial man, aren't you?"

"Well, yeah."

"Dave was the only one of us who had any money."

Of course, there was more to it. Bill told David at the beginning that he'd have to learn the business. After financing the property purchase and construction of a new store in Fort Worth, to be managed by Bill's brother Bob, David spent a month there learning how to marinate the chicken, how to fry it, how to use the cash registers, and how to clean up and close at night. He experienced firsthand the fatigue of a full day's hot and heavy work on a cement floor, and since Church's sold best in rough neighborhoods, he also learned to hand over money at gunpoint.

After getting back from Fort Worth, David met with Bill at Breckenridge Park, and they agreed that everything in the new business should start with philosophy. After hours of discussion, they established the first principle on which the burgeoning corporation would be founded: "There shall never be a policy written that can't be changed." Philosophy firmly agreed upon, David pointed out to Bill that Church's sold 30% more in black and Hispanic neighborhoods and that he had been selling Kirbys in smaller South Texas towns where he'd noticed there were no fast-food establishments. Despite researching chamber of commerce reports and gathering census information, David and Bill had no clue about where to open a store. Finally, they took a philosophical sidestep to the science of random destiny: David chose a page and Bill a line in a towns-of-Texas manual, and they came up with Laredo.

Within days, they found themselves in hundred-degree weather, with no air-conditioning, cruising the only two paved streets in Laredo. Bill pointed out a prime store location on Guadalupe Street, but it presented two complications: a residence stood on it, and it wasn't for sale. The Hispanic owner was taking it easy on his front porch; his five kids ran wild. While Bill slept in the car, David got out, dressed in tee-shirt and jeans, and struck up a conversation, first about the heat, then about Laredo, and then about how dangerous Guadalupe Street traffic was for kids. "I'd get off of this street with them kids," David offered.

"Well, I've been thinking about it. Me and my wife had bought a lot. It's two blocks back here. We're going to build on it."

"Is that right? Maybe we could help you." David couldn't believe his luck. "Hey, show me the lot."

The man came off the porch and called the kids, and the seven of them marched two blocks back on dirt streets, with nothing around to look at.

"Yeah, this is my lot."

"I'll tell you what. We'll buy the house you are living in now. The only thing is we don't want the house. We will have a mover come in, pick your house up, and transport it to this nice lot." Then and there, David made a deal with the man, on a handshake basis. The entire cost amounted to less than $25,000. By the time Bill woke up, their new corporation had acquired a location for its first store.

"The Laredo store was spectacularly profitable, people standing in a line down Guadalupe Street Friday nights. It was strictly walk up, buy the product, and walk away. Right off the bat, it launched our company." David kept to the baseball metaphor. "Every store we opened in the Rio Grande Valley was a home run."

Bill Church re-conceived his father's system of distributing materials from a central processing station. Developing what Bill called the "single unit concept," each store would place and receive its own orders for flour, shortening, and bread; it would marinate the chicken, fry, and sell it on location; and it would hire its own people and look after the payroll. The stores required management personnel more skilled than Bill had used in the past. David acquired an old house in San Antonio and transformed it into a management school, using the family stores as training sites. Under the new system, Church's Food Service Industry could set up stores anywhere in the country while retaining a central location for training personnel. The company opened new stores in Atlanta, Los Angeles, Kansas City, and Dayton, cities where regional headquarters were eventually established.

The company grew fast enough to begin forming divisions. David developed a program he dubbed the "Critical Path," which had a sort of evangelistic ring to it but was in fact a precisely plotted year-long schedule for coordinating real estate acquisition, construction, hiring and training, quality control, and finances. The goal was to open a new store each month. David's primary role was to recruit and train managers and crews ahead of store openings. A training center had been built and a rigid nine-week course had been established in order to maintain high efficiency and quality products.

By 1969 Church's Food Service Industry had created thirty stores, which, after negotiations, were merged with the eleven family stores, primarily in San Antonio. E.F. Hutton & Co. underwrote the promising new company, and Church's Fried Chicken became the first San Antonio-based company to go public. Its stock became a darling of the New York Stock Exchange, opening at $17.50 a share and jumping to $32.00 twenty-four hours later. David's early investments, including the original thousand shares scratched out on 50¢ stationery and given as a somewhat pitiful thank-you, rocketed in value.

Over the following four years, despite the painful complications of the Vietnam War and of civil rights and other social movements, Church's Fried Chicken continued its rapid expansion. Stores were burned down or occupied in Atlanta, Chicago, and L.A. At the same time, Church's was being honored for creating businesses and job opportunities in low-income neighborhoods. There were even suspicions in minority neighborhoods that Church's was part of a government plot to make their population infertile by putting chemicals in the marinade.

Emerging and intensifying disagreements with Bill led David to take a ten-year sabbatical before his return as CEO and board chairman. He gave three reasons for leaving: he wanted the freedom to sell Church's stock, which he couldn't do as a company officer and stockholder; he grew intolerant of Bill's newfound obsession with Scientology; finally, he was passed over for the position of president, one he felt that he had earned, not to mention that it had been promised to him. Bill's presidential choice of another friend was the final straw. David started a new company called Entre Nous and helped launch the restaurant chain 1776 Inc.; he acquired two radio stations; and he continued to be involved in real estate and land development. He became a consultant, investor, and mentor in numerous business startups. Most importantly, he pursued his vision of transforming his ranch from juniper-choked desert into an Eden of springs, creeks, ponds, grasses, and mixed trees. By nature incapable of retiring to become perhaps a golfer and country clubber, he began joining environmental groups, initiating causes, and serving on the boards of nature and wildlife organizations. His involvement with one of these, the American Zoo and Aquarium Association, precipitated some of his greatest publicity and controversy.

The Vermilion Flycatcher at Little Mexico

DAVID BACKED up his tan pickup to a stockpile of pipes and other recyclable building and fencing materials near Little Mexico, the ranch living quarters for up to four Mexican workers at a time. He needed a steel pipe for a new gate that Scott Grote, Selah's operations manager, planned to construct at Windsong. David slid the pipe onto the truck bed. Corey, a medium-sized mixed-breed stray, now official ranch dog—a rags-to-riches story in his own right—was always relegated to the back. To him, objects on the truck bed, such as capricious pipes, were not to be trusted.

A small scarlet bird with black wings dropped out of the shade of an oak and into the angled sunlight. It looked as if its flight program had been scrambled or it was trying to imitate the aimless dancing of a butterfly. The bird was entirely new to me, but then so were others: its cousin, the scissortail flycatcher who hovered vertically over a fence, long tail streaming as from a kite, or the black-bellied whistling ducks, red-footed, perched in a live oak to peer quizzically at drivers entering Johnson City on the Miller Creek Road. I'd had no idea that the Hill Country was so avifauna-affluent. I asked David about the stunning red and black bird. The name escaped him, but he assured me that Margaret would come up with it at dinner later that evening.

I'd often ride with David and talk while he performed countless chores. He was invariably on cruise control when multitasking. Besides loading the pipe that evening, he had come to Little Mexico to water saplings grown under an arbor that protected them from direct sun. Every time I'd visited the ranch, he had doted over the trees and grasses, particularly those produced by his recovery and cultivation of seed, the process of nurturing nature. This sort of passion—scattering mud filled with bald cypress seeds in a newly created lake or planting a cottonwood sprig that in only twelve years grows into the tallest tree on the ranch—requires a decade or more before the enjoyment of any reward. It's an investment in the transformative power of trees and grasses, and David would be the first to say that anyone can do it at virtually no cost, but it takes nurturing.

"Nurturing," in all its permutations, has been a key word in Bamberger's psyche, something of Hes' naturalist spirit infused in his own. David loves to invent words, one being "Nurturey," a fusion of *nurture* and *nursery,* for a steel mesh corral designed to protect seedlings from foraging wildlife. The "Nurturey" is set up on Selah's "Nature Trail," which includes the arboretum. But the whole concept of nurturing goes beyond land stewardship. It also has served as a *modus operandi* as over the decades David has "cultivated" business partners, employees, restaurant managers and crews—and now volunteers, educators, and ranch managers, whom he and Margaret treat as the Selah family.

Under the arbor, David grows Lacey and chinquapin oaks, desert willow, Texas ash, Carolina buckthorn, rough-leaf dogwood, big-toothed maple, and the endangered Texas snowbell. He handed me the hose to help with the watering while he selected three trees as silent auction items for the Family Day Fundraiser. Black-chinned hummingbirds were busy at the trumpet vine at the end of the arbor, near the gray farmhouse with its galvanized roof, runoff stains accentuating the gutters. The Little Mexico farmhouse, constructed by Gus Uecker in the 1890s, is listed as a historic building. Apparently Uecker erected the first windmill in the county and was the first in the area to have a riding cultivator.

The Mexican workers were part of the Selah infrastructure, and I tried to imagine what their lives were like. Raul, Poncho, and Tony came from San Luis de la Paz in the central state of Guanajuato and Maestro, traveling all the way from Rancho Monte Cristo in Suchiate near the Guatemalan boarder, all leaving their families for several months at a stretch. Raul, the oldest, had been working at Selah for twenty-five years. Beside the Little Mexico house is the Green Rotunda, a sifting facility for funneling oryx into separate pens where they can be loaded on trailers or given veterinary attention. The females and their young are fenced to the north in the broad open African Kleingrass area called "The Sahara." The males roam a smaller pasture south of the house. Beyond this pasture, the land rises toward the highest point on the ranch, 1,901 feet. This spot must be both pleasant and exotic for the workers. How would they describe to quizzical friends and family back in Mexico their months with oryx, dama gazelles, Spanish sheep, and axis deer?

David began talking about the Mexicans, whom I'd met while setting up rented tables with them for the Family Day Fundraiser. I'd also watched them cut stone for the base of the George Beere Greenhouse and seen the ingenious buildings, including the Recycle Cabin, they'd constructed with recovered materials. They worked in near silence, speaking only short Spanish phrases and sentences in lowered voices, as they positioned and cemented pieces of shaped limestone. While the Mexicans working at Selah do have working papers, David adamantly defended illegal aliens. "They keep this country going. They are our restaurant workers, maids, baby sitters, garbage removers, fruit pickers, and construction gangs. They are husbands and wives just working hard to raise kids and support families, and yet Congress is under pressure to legislate against them. It's a joke. America can't function without them." This position is in striking contrast to former presidential candidate Pat Buchanan's advocacy of a 2,000-mile wall along the Rio Grande River and the Southwestern border of the United States, an idea that still strongly appeals to many conservatives. If anyone could do a beautiful job of it, using native stone, it would be Mexicans such as those at Selah.

Soon after making the three major land purchases that formed Selah, David found himself hiring itinerant laborers who came around in trucks offering to work or were recommended by neighbors. A number of them became regulars. Twice over a thirty-five year period, the illegal aliens were granted amnesty and were free to work where they chose, but those who had worked at Selah stayed and even recruited family members.

Earlier, Scott Grote, his wife Melissa, and their precocious young children, Willow and Grey, had busily unloaded a week's groceries in Little Mexico's kitchen. The Mexicans had a Sony television in a common room, and other appliances too. Their laundry hung not far from David's saplings. They had gorgeous views of a small savannah-like plateau and of the large white and russet oryx, of Saharan descent. The Mexicans made slightly above minimum wage, but they were in a position to save their income, since room, board, and transportation, including that to and from Mexico, were provided, along with legal documents.

I helped David spread Amdro over erupting circles of sand on Little Mexico's lawn. Amdro is a poison that dutiful fire ants bring unwittingly into the mound to please their queen. I still have scars on my ankles after blundering into fire ant mounds behind the Selah office in Pleasant Valley. I thought I'd somehow strolled into a patch of stinging nettles, so common in Europe. I learned the hard way that fire ants inflict an entirely different degree of misery.

In youthful exuberance, Corey took off after a powerful male oryx that lowered its head to face him. The oryx is the only antelope with the fabled capacity to kill a lion, and Corey was in the middle of a very serious mistake. Oryx are volatile. On occasion they have killed each other at Selah, and they killed a white-tail deer that David put in their pasture. The young deer thought that he, too, was an oryx; he should have been wary. Further evidence of oryx violence is the snapped-off horns on some of the males. But David is also volatile. Corey quickly felt the full force of his temper as the seventy-seven year old rushed down the road and jumped a water crossing to subdue the dog. He didn't hit Corey but certainly hollered him into cowering paralysis. The high crime for any ranch dog is aggression against other animals, a habit that Corey would have to unlearn.

The sun was falling on the far side of Little Mexico, bathing the russet markings of the oryx in fresh springtime light and warmth. Corey's oryx crossed the caliche road back into a pasture with other males, a large axis deer accompanying them. The deer, a native of India, stood serenely in the shadows, his elaborate rack a peculiar contrast to the simple elegance of the oryx's curved horns. David's composure returned as quickly as his rage had flashed. He sang show songs as we stopped at Catfish Tank to close the drainage gate at the base of the dam. The tank was lower than David liked aesthetically, and the fundraiser would bring three hundred people to savor the landscape and value the efforts at Selah.

In many ways, David acted like a big kid full of tireless energy. He looked at me and said, "You're the philosopher. What animal has the most fun?"

"Swallows? Otters? Dolphins?" I offered.

"We do, people!" he insisted. That answer hadn't occurred to me. He went on singing while I enumerated to myself doubts about his choice.

We had just crossed into the western section of Selah, over three slopes and past Little Mexico and the endangered species area a little north of its center. This piece of land, the last major acquisition in the composition of Selah, is shaped something like Texas would be if it were somehow squashed in an east-west vice. It is contiguous with a large ranch owned by the Heaths, the family who eventually sold the 2,043 acres to David.

The Heath family has a relatively long history in Texas, owning vast tracts in Blanco County. In the early 1970s, David had gotten to know Mr. Heath, the former U.S. ambassador to Sweden, and had consulted with the family for years. Leroy, Selah's engineer, and his family had worked for the Heaths all their lives. In fact, Leroy's property formed a kind of island in the middle of the vast Heath acreage. David had made a handshake agreement with Mr. Heath to buy some of his land, but they hadn't reached a formal accord on how much of the ranch would be involved. David recalled, "I was on business in Greensboro, North Carolina, and I missed my plane to San Antonio, which was supposed to get me in on time to meet with Mr. Heath that very day. I put in a call to him at his law office to explain that I'd be late. The secretary asked who was calling, and I said, 'David Bamberger. I had an appointment with Mr. Heath this afternoon.' She said, 'I'll let you talk to Mr. Davis.' Mr. Heath's law partner came on the phone and said, 'Mr. Bamberger, Mr. Heath passed away.' The guy died the day I was going to see him about that deal."

After the funeral, David, still interested in the purchase, got in touch with the family. They said that nothing could be done for at least three years; the estate had to be settled, the operation of the ranch arranged, and taxes considered. When that period was over, David renewed contact with the Heaths and finally reached an agreement.

At a legal session at his San Antonio office, David organized a three-way deal designed to minimize taxes. The Bulverde ranch would be sold to a Dr. Williamson, and that money would go to the Heath family in partial payment for 2,043 acres in Johnson City. With the lawyers, Dr. Williamson, and the Heaths assembled around the table, Cynthia Heath, the oldest daughter, announced, "I can't sell it!" and bolted. Her family in pursuit on the city streets, the rest of the assembly was left gazing at each other in dismay. David recalled, "Boy, that was a tense moment. And she was right, of course." More than an hour passed, and Dr. Williamson and the lawyers shifted uneasily in their chairs. The Heath family tracked down Cynthia and restored order, if not reason, where hysteria and sudden regret had held the upper hand. They filed back, resigned, into the boardroom.

The principal components of Selah had finally been assembled, the Heath property being a prize. It had been much better cared for than the Carter land. Journalist Suzy Banks put the extent of the Bamberger Ranch into perspective, at least for eastern-minded people, when she wrote that Selah was approximately a third the size of Manhattan.

Somehow my impression of land ownership had been different on my arrival in the Hill Country. I'd thought, naively, that the land still consisted of old family ranches belonging to and maintained by the likes of Leroy Petri. I was learning that vast properties belonged to owners of media conglomerates, computer companies, NFL football teams, and dotcom sites. Some ranches dwarfed Selah. Some had Learjet airports that could accommodate a Boeing 737. Some were already in the hands of developers. I began seeing these properties and meeting their owners.

After David and I returned from checking the levels of the tanks at Little Mexico, David served me a shamefully large iced Jim Rhoades. Margaret was already dressed. She reported finding sixty-four different types of wildflowers just in the lawn surrounding the house. Some days she had less energy and stayed close to home. As David fed Corey, I described the little red bird with black wings at Little Mexico. As David had promised, she did know it, a vermilion flycatcher, not uncommon at the ranch, though I saw only the one during my two-month stay. She said, "It's an adorable bird, one of my favorites. The eyeline and wings are brown, and it looks almost black in some light. The rest is an orange-red so bright that the first time you see him, actually every time after for that matter, you gasp. He holds the feathers on his head up a little so that they catch the light." She explained further, "And his fitful flight shows up his brilliant color for the females."

David, Margaret, and I drove the caliche roads and rattled over cattle guards out Selah's back gate and through the Heath ranch, past Leroy's farm. The farm stood in a valley below the ridge, his crops forming flawless rows, his equipment carefully housed, and his buildings impeccably maintained. We were on our way to a neighbor's annual barbecue, thrown for Blanco neighbors and friends as well as friends and family from different parts of the country. The ranch owner came from Denver, although his wife had grown up in San Antonio. David had loaned picnic tables that he had rented for the Family Day Fundraiser the next day. The Mexicans would pick them up in the morning amid the post-party debris. Although this was a private barbecue, cars had been parked along the drive as if we were coming to a country fair. A wooden bridge crossed the runoff creek from a pond called the "Swamp Angel," and tables were so packed with people that we had trouble finding a seat, finally getting an invitation to join a jocular group from Denver. I began to understand the sort of event this would be. Lights looped down from the trees and across a catered barbecue area in a wood building that could easily have served as a restaurant. It was connected to a private dance hall with a stage and a bar. The people with whom we shared a table were friends flown in to enjoy smoked turkey, ribs, sausage, and brisket smothered in spectacularly spicy sauce and garnished with jalapeños, which everyone agreeably neutralized with frozen margaritas.

I was tipsy in no time, partly from outsider's nervousness and partly because the margaritas, so rare back in Paris, were irresistible. Margaret drifted off among friends, who were astonished to see her looking so well. They'd had word-of-mouth news that she'd been in dreadful condition at the Fredericksburg Hospital. David held court at our table, launching into oft-told Church's Fried Chicken stories for the rapt Coloradoans. I sat quietly absorbing the springtime night filled with talk, laughter, and country music at a ranch owned by an extremely wealthy man I hadn't met before. I could not fathom the cost of such a party.

After the people at our table had left for the dance hall, connected to a private saloon, David introduced me to some of the local land owners, in particular his friend Benini, a dramatic-looking Italian with a full silvery beard and long hair that gave him a likeness to Walt Whitman in later life, if you can imagine Walt with a heavy Italian accent. Benini, an accomplished painter and sculptor with a flair for *haute cuisine,* and Lorraine, his wife, had created the Benini Foundation and Sculpture Park on 140 acres that had once belonged to Lyndon B. Johnson. Now well-known locally, and increasingly so throughout the state, the ranch has a guesthouse, studio, gallery, library, and a sculpture garden including mostly monumental abstract pieces set in the native grasses with oaks, junipers, and rugged hills in the background. Benini holds a speaker's series, primarily on art, but it ranges to include talks by David on the "Art of Land Stewardship" and Selah administrator Colleen Gardner's "The Beauty and the Buzz . . . The Art of Beekeeping."

Two of the Heath sisters showed up, radiating in the dark, both very attractive and dressed up in Texas outfits as if on a movie set. They were delighted to see David and asked about Margaret. Later in the dance hall, I was getting one last margarita. As big as the hall was, with a bar and a stage, the dance floor packed, there was little room to maneuver. I knew that Margaret would want to leave soon. In the evening she tired early. I was taken off guard when one guest had the poor judgment to ask me to dance. I couldn't compete with the vermilion flycatcher's dance on air. She said, "Girls are nice to guys who dance with them."

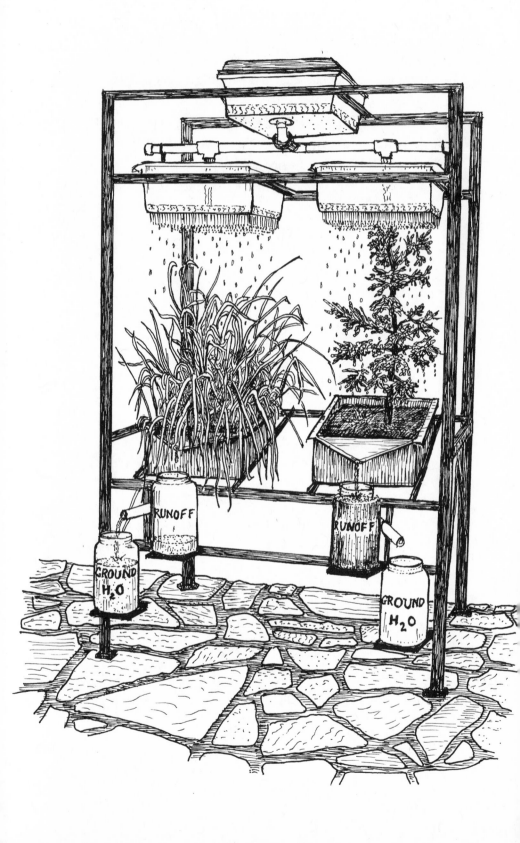

Grasses and the D6 Caterpillar

MOST PEOPLE in and around the Hill Country are steeped in the history of the area's environmental damage, which coincided with settlement. Nineteenth-century German and Irish settlers discovered what they thought were rich grass-covered hills and meadows and imagined productive grazing land. But while the high-quality grasses weren't exactly a mirage, their ecology was far more delicately balanced than anyone knew, the topsoil being thin and vulnerable. A natural balance of periodic grass fires and migrations of grazing bison herds had helped produce a grassland savannah that supported deer, turkey, quail, prairie chicken, and songbirds. Herds of bison, emblematic in the lore of the American west, stretched nearly a hundred miles and passed through the region as recently as the mid-nineteenth century. They grazed in huge swaths and weren't picky about their forage, relegating native Ashe juniper, known locally as cedar, mainly to canyons. But the bison would pass through only once every two or three years and never remained in one area long enough to damage their own habitat. In addition, natural wildfires would burn off saplings and cactuses while fertilizing the soil for native grasses. The land appeared so appealing to the settlers, some coming through agencies in Germany and some from the hills of Alabama, Tennessee, and Kentucky, that they were willing to take their chances against attacks by Apaches and later the fiercer Comanches. By the second half of the nineteenth century, fences and farms were built, fires were put out to protect structures and the livestock, and bison were systematically killed off. Cattle, horses, pigs, sheep, and goats began to overgraze the native grasses, and, to make matters worse, short-stemmed grasses were introduced for forage, but their shallow root structures were insufficient for retaining soil. During World War I, the federal government struck the fatal blow by subsidizing meat production in the area. The increased grazing and hoof action destroyed root systems and stripped the earth bare, resulting, as droughts came, in the infamous Dust Bowl, followed by severe erosion when typically torrential rainfall at last returned. Subsequent damage from the mohair sheep industry capped the environmental disaster. The forestry service postulates that it takes five hundred years to produce an inch of topsoil; thus, thousands of years of topsoil were lost in a matter of mere decades. Limestone outcroppings and shallow-rooted Ashe junipers, prickly pear cactuses, and greenbrier replaced the former grasslands. Soon after, springs vanished, and creeks dried up.

The Carter Ranch was "the sorriest piece of land in Blanco County" because it was essentially wall-to-wall Ashe juniper. It had no lakes, ponds, or running creeks. David contends that it supported only forty-eight species of birds; that one cow required forty-one acres; and disgruntled hunters who bought $3,000 leases were dressing deer at fifty-five pounds, the weight of some medium-sized dogs. David prefaces his after-habitat-restoration statistics with calculated modesty: "This may sound like boasting" or "I don't mind saying I'm proud." He then delivers some mind-boggling figure. Even without David's salesmanship, one can readily see the splendor of what was accomplished at the ranch by the clearing out of Ashe juniper and the planting of native grasses. He tells audiences, "I try to convince people that sensible land stewardship is not just good for Mother Nature and the quality of life we all have here but it is also good economics. We now have two hundred mother cows. We can run an animal unit to 18 acres. We have, at the last bird count, one hundred and eighty three species. Last year we earned $43,000 in hunting leases. Last weekend we had turkey hunters who paid $5,000. You know how many they shot? Five. You could go to the supermarket and buy five hundred of them for that kind of money. But the city folks liked being in the country."

The statistics that the Bamberger Ranch uses are convincing. A twelve-inch-diameter juniper will consume at least twelve gallons of water per day out of the soil. The interception rate for a one-inch rain is 26% in the dense branches with their scale-like leaves, and at the bottom, where other plant life is shaded out and the organic ground material forms a barrier, less than 20% ever gets into the earth. The vast majority of junipers on the original Carter Ranch had to go.

It is one thing to hear statistics and another to see for oneself the effects of juniper overgrowth. At one point or another, Selah visitors are led to the "Rain Machine," which is set up at one of the numerous outdoor classrooms, this one located on the shore of Madrone Lake near the beginning of the Nature Trail. Calling it a "Rain Machine" annoys Margaret, who as an educator and naturalist understandably prefers accuracy. She warned me on several occasions not to be confused. "It is a rain simulator."

I decided that it all depends on who is demonstrating the simulator and to whom. For David it will always be the more whimsical "Rain Machine," whether he is operating it for the San Antonio Foundation or for middle-school kids. The audience sits in rows at lakeside tables while David, the man who was responsible for selling 43,000 Kirby sweepers, demonstrates a seven-foot, forest-green steel rack with a four-gallon reservoir at the top and white PVC pipe that distributes water evenly to two plastic receptacles resembling dish-washing basins, except that both are evenly perforated by a grid of four hundred hypodermic needles producing an evenly distributed shower. Placed directly below the needle-filled basins, but at a slight tilt, are two more trays, one with bare soil and young Ashe juniper saplings and the other with a healthy tuft of little bluestem grass. Both have thermometers, the Ashe juniper tray registering seventeen degrees warmer, the difference affecting the survival of all kinds of insects and other organisms that live in grasses, as opposed to under junipers. The containers each have a funnel at soil level and jars at the opening labeled "Run-Off," and at the bottom of the trays more PCV pipe leads to jars labeled "Ground H_2O." A valve below the reservoir releases the water to simulate a one-inch rainfall, which for the audience takes less than ten minutes.

During the simulated shower, David holds up a clump of little blue-stem, its abundant beard-like root system almost directly proportional to the tuft of stems that would extend above ground. We learn that the roots could be strung out over nine miles. It's easy to see how the stems gently absorb the rainfall while the fibrous roots allow the water to go into the earth and replenish the aquifer as they hold the soil in place. The Hill Country aquifers are formed out of Edwards limestone, which in the hills of Selah makes up a 125-foot layer of honeycombed rock.

The Rain Machine performs dutifully. The audience watches the shower hitting the bare ground under Ashe junipers and pouring down deep brown into the "Run-Off" jar while the "Ground H_2O" remains all but empty. Predictably, the grass tray produces minimal runoff while providing a healthy full jar of ground water. David picks it up, looks directly at me, takes a large gulp, and wipes his smile with his cuff. "The purest water you can drink," he declares. "We use it at the ranch house, and everyone who lives on Selah uses it." Half a century earlier David was vacuuming couples' beds and showing them their own skin. Now he is the snake oil salesman for the environment, but this product, if properly applied, truly works miracles.

Most people don't think of how fundamental grasses are to our lives. To begin with, many of the grains we eat or use as feed—rice, corn, and wheat—are species of grass. Grasses provide forage, wildlife cover, sod, and protection against erosion. At Selah, we see the value of grasses in replenishing aquifers. David has said that "the soul of Selah is glimpsed in her grasses" and that Madrone Lake is Selah's "heart." One could take those two metaphors and make difficult extrapolations about which comes first, the "soul" or the "heart." In the case of habitat restoration at Selah, the soul came first; the story of water followed. David explains, "You can spend hundreds of millions of dollars building dams, diversion ditches, and berms, but there is no better conservation tool than grass."

While the story of Selah is the story of water and grasses, it is also the story of machines. *The Austin Chronicle* ran a picture of David supporting himself on axe handles in each hand, one foot on a stack of chain-saws.

Ad-libbing with reporter Suzy Banks, who wrote the article "A Call to the Wild," he claimed to have worn out thirty-eight chain-saws. "It could have been twenty-two. All I knew was it had been a load of them," David reported. "She called my hand. She said, 'Let's see it.' So I said, 'Get in the truck' and drove to the part of the ranch we call Leroy's office. I knew he had a bunch of those things thrown back in there. I pulled them out and made that stack out there, and she said, 'That's enough! That's enough! I believe you.' She took that picture."

David's assertion that he has cleared over 3,000 acres that had been nothing but Ashe juniper has been called into question. It was a figure he gave early on when his work at Selah had begun to gain recognition, and he sticks to it. The 3,000-acre Carter property was covered in Ashe juniper, and later properties that at one point reached 6,400 acres also had their share of it and needed clearing. Juniper produces its berries tirelessly, and the re-emergence of the tree is virtually unending. When the Mexicans finish shaping and cementing stone for new terraces and buildings, they are out on the ranch clearing junipers with lopping shears and chainsaws. The 3,000 acres of nothing-but-juniper has probably been cleared at least twice over.

It's essential to point out that juniper is a native Texas tree, and David would be the first to say that the land should be sculpted and certain juniper brakes preserved to promote diversity, create wildlife cover, and provide the singular nesting material required by the endangered golden-cheeked warbler, who cleverly binds strips of juniper bark with caterpillar webs to make a nest in hardwoods like Spanish oak. The caterpillars hatch at the same time as the warblers, providing food for the little birds right at their doorstep. The cut junipers are useful as erosion barriers, firewood, and most famously, resilient cedar posts for fencing. Juniper is even used in soap and perfume.

Donna, David, and the Bamberger kids basically camped out when they stayed at Selah. The one well provided undrinkable water. The ranch house was all but forsaken, full of bullet holes. No one had lived there except deer hunters who leased the place from mid-fall to mid-winter.

One of David's first deer hunters was Charley Duke, an astronaut who had landed on the moon. He came recently to Selah to hear Jane Goodall talk, and he called out, "Bamberger. Charley Duke. Boy, has this place ever changed." There was no shortage of hunting stories, including one about the arrest of Selah hunters who strayed onto a neighbor's property and shot deer reserved for Henry Kissinger. When David asked a lawyer's advice, saying that the game warden, county sheriff, and county judge had arrested them, the response was, "You might as well be going up against the Ayatollah."

Besides having a ranch overrun by junipers, two wells with gyp water, and uncounted miles of broken-down fences, David hired as manager a ranch hand whom he described as "old-school: pickup, coon dog, and bottle of beer," all of which gave a finishing touch to the place's dilapidation. The manager lived in the house that is now in Pleasant Valley. He was dishonest, stealing from the Bambergers and, even worse, from the hunters. David quickly replaced him with a couple, John and Patsy Madison.

The rehabilitation of the former Carter property, and later the whole of Selah, began in earnest when David hired twenty-six-year-old Leroy Petri, fresh from the Army Corps of Engineers. The connection was made through Charlie Kuhn, husband of David's secretary, who also ended up in business with David. Leroy was young and eager to please and possessed uncanny engineering gifts based on what David called "just plain-assed common sense." Leroy wanted to know what equipment David wanted, and together they managed to purchase at a public auction a D6 series Caterpillar bulldozer at the extraordinary bargain price of $20,000. Leroy immediately went to work toppling and uprooting junipers on the crests and bottoms of hills. The slopes had to be worked with chain-saws and lopping sheers.

While cutting a juniper near ground level kills that individual, it is nearly impossible to eradicate junipers altogether, nor is it desirable. David discovered that every time one large juniper was removed, thirty-seven replaced it over a period of four years. Beneath the trees are thousands of berries; exposed to rain and sunlight, they come to vigorous life when the larger tree is removed. Saplings must be cut or reduced through prescribed burns.

David claims that the biggest mistake he made in the early days was going to Douglas King Seed Company in San Antonio, the major seed dealer in the southwest. He recalls, "I went to the Douglas King Seed Company in my half-ton pickup, looking for native seed. The seller looked at my list and asked, 'Mr. Bamberger, what are you driving?' 'My pickup.' He looked out the window and said two things: 'First, you better go get an eighteen wheeler. This seed isn't going to fit on a pickup truck. Second, I don't have this seed for you. But I'll start searching other dealers in Texas, and you ought to come back with your stock trailer in ten days. I'll try to get as much as can.' I spent thousands on native grass seed. I taught a lot of people not to do that. Don't make that mistake. I can teach them how to gather seed for little or nothing."

Leroy welded together a spring-toothed cultivator and hooked it to the back of a tractor. Once Leroy had cleared a piece of land, David followed with the tractor, "scarifying" the earth. Conventional wisdom was that, for fear of erosion, you didn't want to turn up the rocks, soil, and stumps, but David was convinced that he could form mini-terraces and create seedbeds. Stones flew up from the cultivator trailing behind the tractor and pelted the back of his head as he rode the hills, resolved to contour his land for the grass. After scarifying the ground, he and his sons would spread grass seed on windy weekend days in February and March and then work it into the soil by dragging, of all things, juniper branches attached to the tractor.

David reports that the soil conservation agent and others had been skeptical about the method because the Hill Country didn't have just one-inch showers or gentle rains but was instead notorious for five- or six-inch deluges. They were convinced that the seed would wash off the hills. The agent said, "Now that you've denuded the place, you'll get a five-inch rain, and your expensive seed will be washed into the valley." The agent had been right about the rainfall. It was strong enough to wash out twenty to thirty feet of mini-terraces in just a few places. But for the most part the little terraces held the soil and seed in place. In late March, David saw the hills on his ranch completely transformed by fine green sprouts. A local friend had a Piper Tri-Pacer and flew David over his ranch. It was breathtaking. The grass looked like it had been planted with a grain drill.

While the land was being cleared of juniper and then seeded, the problem of accessing potable water had yet to be solved. David couldn't find a driller that satisfied him. He found that drillers in the area used a rig called a sputter, a cable tool that wound up a two-hundred-pound hunk of iron with a point and let it drop. They dug a well by pounding a hole through earth and rock. David learned of rotary air rigs and found that they were manufactured in Texas. The mast and the rotary drill were mounted on a crane carrier, a huge truck with a cab for one person. The rig resembled the long fire trucks that require a second driver, in the rear, to steer the back wheels. Complementing the resemblance was the thirty-foot mast, a scaffold for directing the drill that would rise on hydraulic pistons like fire ladders.

David had visions of going into the well drilling business. He strayed from his golden rule of buying only secondhand equipment and wrote a check for $200,000. He ordered a rotary air drill rig powered by two Gardner-Denver air compressors and hydraulic stabilizers. You could drive to a site in the Hill Country, push a button, level the crane carrier, raise the mast, and begin drilling within an hour or two. David, basically ignorant of the whole drilling business, found that there were details that he hadn't considered. He had to purchase an expensive drill stem and then a $6,000 diamond drill bit from Hughes Tool in Houston. Besides, with rotary drilling, water had to be pumped into the hole to cool, lubricate, and remove debris. David was forced to purchase a water tank truck as well. The acquisitions pyramided to a quarter-of-a-million-dollar investment, all provoked by the gyp water at Selah.

David asked his secretary Myrna if she thought that her husband Charlie would like to be a partner in the water well drilling business. Next day, her answer was a resounding yes. David offered $8,000 a year and 25% of the profit. Charlie knew nothing about well drilling either, but he had run bulldozers, backhoes, and graders. "We didn't know geology and all that. Well, hell, we didn't know anything. We just tore out into it. The company was called Hill Country Water. But the deal I had was that once Charlie learned how to operate the thing and when there was a slowdown in business, he'd come up to my ranch and drill wells all over it. I didn't even know you had to get a permit to drill holes for a well. I didn't even give it any thought. Shit, just do it."

The rig was called a Gardner-Denver 1500, which meant that it could drill to fifteen hundred feet. Trying to economize, David bought only five hundred feet of drill stem. Selah, particularly the original 3,000 acres, is in a part of Blanco County called by the state a critical groundwater area. There just isn't any water in the upper formations. Once you drill through the Edwards limestone, you reach the harder limestone formations that do not retain much water. You have to get down into rocks of the Trinity aquifer, which are deeper than five hundred feet.

While the wells on Selah were coming up empty, the well drilling business started rolling, with more work than Charlie could handle in areas that kept expanding despite no more advertising than some mini-boards in certain neighborhoods. Charlie learned about keeping logs, though he never filed them. Also, at the time there was a controversy over lignite mining in the Austin area, and coincidentally, Margaret and some of her friends had formed "Lignite Watch" to thwart local strip mining and the subsequent use of lignite in power plants by Austin, San Antonio, and the Lower Colorado River Authority. David, aware of this controversy, but decades from knowing Margaret, asked Charlie to notify him if he ran into veins of lignite. The mining company might have wanted lignite closer to San Antonio, and David dreamed of securing mineral rights and making an easy million. Fortunately for David's environmental record, Charlie found only six-foot veins, not worth rolling back the earth to strip-mine it out.

Charlie was a heavy-set, boisterous guy, and a terrible businessman. An agent approached him at a drilling site and asked for his license. In a kind of odd rerun of David's used car business in high school, neither Charlie nor David had a clue that a license was required. It turned out that well drillers had to have site permits, official logs submitted to the state, and licenses issued after a year-long apprenticeship and the passing of various tests.

"We were ignorant of the law," David told me. "They just shut us down. I don't want a quarter-of-a-million-dollars worth of equipment rusting while it takes a year for Charlie to work under another guy. I went to a fellow that we met up in Burnet, Texas. He was a licensed driller with a sputter rig. I showed him the Gardner-Denver and struck a deal with him: 'Charlie will do all the work.' He'd just have to come on the site once a day and hang his license on the rig."

Meanwhile, Charlie had drilled one dry hole after another on the ranch. David's fondest hope was to have a good well near the house. In a crowning moment of frustration, Charlie managed, while trying to drill that very well, to twist off the $6,000 bit. Leroy came to David and said in his wry Texas deadpan, "Just because you own that rig, them holes you're drilling ain't free."

"You bet your life they ain't free," David answered.

"Well, I've got an idea. My dad told me there's a spring up back there. It's not a good one, but it never went dry during the drought." He took David up and showed him the spring, digging it out with a little pick. "I can case this off and pipe this water. It'll be good water, all you need. I figure for about $1,800 I can put this water down to your house."

David was suspicious. "I couldn't figure out how Leroy was going to bring water down a hill and up a hill and then down a hill and around a hill and come out at the ranch house. I was thinking in terms of airlocks and all the friction in the pipes. I'm not cued into it yet." One of the engineers from Church's came out to the ranch and only confirmed David's doubts. Still, David was faced with two undeniable points: he had no other options, and $1,800 seemed not too big a gamble.

Leroy, eager to prove his idea, drilled out the spring and encased it in cement. He connected the PVC line down to the house without burying it. He spent only $600 and held off ordering the $1,200 cistern, which would be manufactured at a cement plant outside San Antonio. Leroy executed the system three days earlier than expected, leaving David scrambling to reschedule his office appointments and drive up to the ranch to see the water system in action. Patsy Madison heard David coming and ran out of her driveway, holding up a tray of ice cubes. "Mr. Bamberger, look!"

David stopped his truck. "What?"

"Look, Mr. Bamberger. The ice cubes."

"What about them?"

"They're clear!"

The only water on the ranch had been Bloody Mary red and stank. You couldn't drink it, bathe in it, or launder with it. The ranch suddenly had spring water. Leroy dug the channel, buried the pipe, put up the cistern, and completed the plumbing. Over the years other storage was added until, all combined, the ranch got 22,000 gallons of stored water from one spring. Paradoxically, there was another option that David hadn't considered. If he had bought another five hundred feet of drill stem for the Gardner-Denver 1500, the story of water at Selah might have been very different.

With more junipers cleared and more grasses planted and with the grass seed being harvested in autumn along roads and fields, the parched Edwards aquifer was finally filled and brimming. More springs and seeps were discovered, and soon the creeks on the eastside watershed would run year-round. David and Leroy plotted new tasks for the D6 Caterpillar bulldozer.

It would be enough for most ranchers that the D6 would give over thirty years of service, thanks in good part to Leroy's maintenance and mechanical know-how. But the bulldozer also became a model for David's good-stewardship economics: "When I make the statement that anyone can do what I have done regardless of how much money he or she has in the bank, someone always puts up a hand and says, 'All this is wonderful, Mr. Bamberger, but I can't afford a bulldozer.' Now let me tell you how that plays out. If I had enough money to buy 5,500 acres, doesn't it stand to reason that I can go to a public auction and pay $20,000 for a $200,000 bulldozer?

"Every piece of equipment that we've ever had on this ranch has been used. We are using our third motor grader. We never paid over $5,000 for one. We are on our third backhoe, and we never paid over $5,000 for one. The bulldozer we bought had 2,900 hours on it. We paid $20,000. We put 14,000 hours on that bulldozer on this land. If you hire to have that done in this part of Texas, you will spend $1,200,000. Leroy came to me just a few weeks ago, and he said, 'Dave, you know we're not using the dozer much any more. I think it's time to sell it.' Well, I've had that sucker for thirty-five years. Who would want it? He said, 'Well, it will bring $30,000 to $35,000.' We paid $20,000. We got $1,200,000 out of it. And now it's going to bring $30,000. Is that spending a lot of money?" Of course, David neglects to mention that Leroy is a gifted mechanic who gets 500,000 miles out of his trucks. "Now here's the comparison. If you have only enough, Mr. Jones and Mrs. Jones, to buy 5 acres, you don't need to buy a bulldozer. You don't need a tractor and a shredder, Bobcats and all that stuff. You need a chainsaw, a wheelbarrow, axe, hoe, and rake. You do it by hand. If you have enough money to buy 500 or 1,000 acres in this part of Texas, you have enough money to buy a tractor and a few of the attachments that go on it. Everything is relative."

David has never been short on praise for Leroy. I could hear echoes of Bromfield's praise for farmers. "He does so many things that we just don't have the background for, although they are based on rock-solid common sense and the old German work ethic. The farmers and ranchers had to do everything in order to take care of themselves. I've always said I couldn't have created Selah without Leroy."

I've flipped through photo albums that capture the enormity of the cedar-clearing project. Soon afterwards, Leroy carved out the basins for the Carter, Catfish, Little Mexico, Submarine, and Jack Springs tanks, all with earthen dams. The pictures show the D6 bulldozer dwarfed in broad, scarred earth almost impossible to imagine filled with water and healed with grasses. Although basic principles of earthen dams are relatively simple, they require a quality contractor with proven know-how because of the responsibility of owning a safe dam, one that is sure to hold water, and the high initial cost. Leroy said, "Anyone can get on a machine and push dirt up."

Madrone Lake is the centerpiece of Selah. Standing on the Madrone Lake dam, you can see how harmonious with the surrounding land an earthen dam can be, a steep grass slope angled down to the canyon, the dam's base over three hundred feet wide, more than a football field. For every vertical foot, Leroy would need three feet of width at the bottom. An adjacent slope just southwest of the canyon conveniently provided clay for the core of the dam and its lining. When Leroy probed the basin, he found rock that would hold water. Leroy installed a "drawdown and drain device" to automatically maintain Madrone Lake's volume of approximately 150 acre-feet.

I once sat next to Leroy, who gazed serenely at the lake's edge. We said practically nothing to each other. It's hard to know what goes on in a reserved, stoical Texan's mind, though more than likely it's the same inner rankling that any of us has to cope with. But it must be gratifying, even after decades, to have created a large, clear pond in the middle of a critical water area and to see how much richness it adds to the landscape. Making a lake materialize where there had been thick brush, outcroppings, and worn boulders in a creek bed may seem like wizardry, but the principles of earthen dam building are ancient. David says Madrone Lake is the heart of Selah. Leroy says, "If you don't have water in this part of the country, you don't have anything."

Grassmasters and Beef Candy Bars

IN MAY ON Selah's highest points, where the fossil grounds are and the ledge with tracks left by the fearsome *Acrocanthosaurus*, lace and nipple cactuses put out gaudy flowers, purple-pink and yellow with red, respectively. The trees that David planted are in full leaf, with his trademark steel mesh corrals protecting them from foragers. We drove the Post Oak Trail where it passes under the highlines along a power company easement, and Corey barked at a heard of Nubian goats but admirably refrained from attacking them. The goats, sold for their meat, are the most profitable livestock on the ranch, all things considered. On the same range, we came to David's cattle, which are solid, mid-sized stock with a slight shoulder hump, sweet faces, and varied coloring: some a rich and unusual solid reddish brown with darker marks. The variation of coloring and even morphology from cow to cow is indicative of "composite" cattle, in this case a cross that includes one-eighth North American bison. David's scheme to produce a new breed of cattle extended back to Selah's earliest days and was a part of his irrepressible drive to try something different, something he has admitted is "half-goofy" (Belsie). In creating Selah, David followed his idol Bromfield in habitat restoration and in finding bright, like-minded ranch workers, but a 5,500-acre Texas Hill Country ranch posed a different set of practical challenges than did a 385-acre farm in the rolling northern Ohio hills.

In *Pleasant Valley,* Bromfield outlined one of his primary goals for Malabar Farm: self-sufficiency. After a careful search for someone younger who could facilitate his vision of habitat restoration on the three Ohio farms he had combined, Bromfield hired Max Drake, not only an exceptional graduate of the state agricultural school but also a man possessed of a mystical rapport with the soil and an uncanny understanding of animals. Bromfield said to him at the time, "I wanted . . . to be on my own land, on an island of security which could be a refuge not only for myself and family but my friends as well." Self-sufficiency or, more broadly, self-reliance, a fixture in early American ideology, equaled well-being for Bromfield, and he was convinced that soil restoration, a healthy rotation of crops, and natural fertilizers would "bear rich dividends" that could be divided among the families living on the farm. Bromfield's provocative model was the farm collective in Russia. He preached a new creed of environmentally sound agricultural practices, which he deeply believed should form the moral and economic backbone of America. Self-sufficiency was achieved at Malabar, but it didn't endure, not because it wasn't possible but because of personal extravagance, the loss of close friends and family, broad changes in farming, and market miscalculations. While in his plan Bromfield made provisions for collective sharing of the farm's products, he also in reality built a stately, multi-gabled mansion overlooking the farm and the valley. There he regularly hosted high-society affairs, the most famous of which was the 1945 wedding of Humphrey Bogart and Lauren Bacall.

Like Bromfield, David is a fervent believer in the primacy of planning, whether the "Critical Path" for Church's Fried Chicken or the five-year plans he drew up for the improvement and efficiency of his neighbors' ranches. However, he harbored no illusions about ranch self-sufficiency in Texas. He told his audiences, bluntly: "Here's my testimony: there is not one square inch of the state of Texas that you can purchase at prevailing market prices and pay for with any form of agricultural practice whatsoever. It's impossible. It's sad, but it's impossible. We're now enjoying the best cattle market that we've had in thirty-six years, but it's the same market we had thirty-six years ago. The first truck I bought up here cost $7,200, and the last one cost $27,000. This isn't cattle country in the first place. Mohair is not a big thing anymore, with globalization. You can get mohair out of Asia and Africa and other places. The market for our real estate is for quality of life. The big movement in this part of the world is to have a piece of country land away from the congestion of the big city. Larger ranches are being cut up into smaller and smaller tracts, and this is a threat to Mother Nature."

David has a remarkable record of recruiting talented people who have contributed largely to Selah's success. Just as Bromfield recruited from the local college, David created a team of three Texas A&M University graduates: Buddy Francis handled livestock; Randy Lenz was responsible for wildlife and eventually the oryx program; and Jim Rhoades, an urban arborist, helped establish a healthy diversity of trees on the ranch. Although Leroy had no college education, he proved to be Selah's most valuable asset and thus was a major player on the team. Few universities enjoy the rabid alumni support of Texas A&M. Because its alums are known as "Aggies," David dubbed the ranch help his "cow Aggie," his "deer Aggie," his "tree Aggie," and his "dam Aggie," Leroy qualifying honorifically.

While David was keenly aware that his ranch wouldn't be self-sufficient, he wasn't willing to operate at a loss larger than he had to. He knew that nature was less generous to agriculture in the Texas Hill Country than in other parts of the country. Bromfield wrote:

> There were things I wanted to prove; that worn-out farms could be restored again and if only you farmed the hill country in the proper way, you could grow as much as on any of the flat land where something rich was missing from life.

Likewise, David wanted to make his Hill Country ranch productive, but he faced an even greater challenge. With the restoration of native grasses on Selah, the land could support a larger population of cattle, and later, goats would be added. Still, diets had to be supplemented and grazing closely monitored. Breeding cattle that wouldn't be so be so selective about what they ate and would digest rougher forms of cellulose in their diet was a dream not just for the Hill Country but also for poorer nations with less than ideal pasture land. From the early twentieth century, and occasionally even earlier, ranchers had tried crossing North American bison with cattle and, when successful, they called them "Cattalo."

Notoriously, the bison, which had once numbered somewhere between sixty and a hundred million, had been reduced to herds of only a few hundred. They faced extinction as a result of "sport" and a government program to systematically starve out western American Indians, considered enemies. In the 1920s, an effort was made to revive the bison, and ranchers and Indians kept small herds. Bison that foraged across the plains and even in the mountains possessed desirable characteristics: they were hardy, they endured rough weather, their meat had a lower fat content, they lived longer, and above all they were non-selective, efficient feeders able to survive on less hospitable land. These traits would be advantageous in cattle, but early crosses of bison bulls with bovine females produced infertile offspring.

In Luther, Montana, a pioneering rancher named James Burnett had a neighbor with a small herd of bison that he pastured with some cattle. Burnett had observed that his neighbor's heifers were producing hybrid offspring, but while the calves survived, the heifers died in the process. Burnett was convinced that he could produce a fertile hybrid without killing the heifers. In an interview for the *Beefalo Nickel*, Burnett explained,

> Of course, to start with, I didn't do any better than that. In fact, I did a little worse. I went from about 1958 until 1962 before I got a live progeny. I had a lot of dead cows and dead calves. Somebody asked me why I continued. Well I told him, "I suppose it's through stupidity more than anything else. . . ."

> In 1962, I got five live progeny, one of which happened to be the mother of 903. 903 is the bull that Basolo took to California that started the "Beefalo."

Burnett began solving his difficulties with lethal crosses when he shifted from the plains-type bison to mountain bison that he had bought from

Indians in Browning, Montana. Mountain bison are a smaller, shaggier subspecies that can range as high as 12,000 feet and forage at mountain timberlines. Burnett bred a bovine bull to a female mountain bison, engendering three fertile cows and two infertile bulls. He then bred a bison bull with one of the fertile cows, producing a fertile three-quarters bison bull. It was this bull that Bud Basolo, an opportunist with a flair for marketing, used in 1966 to produce his line of hybrids.

In 1973, David sent one of his sons and his new cow Aggie, Buddy Francis, to California to investigate the Beefalo. David remembered, "The guy in California did a marvelous job of marketing, announcing he was going to save the world by crossing the cow with the buffalo. He got on the Johnny Carson show and jetted around America. My guys thought it was worth looking into. I asked each of them to give me a report. It turned out that the biggest thing wrong with Beefalo was Basolo. I put a large amount of money into it, buying some of the Beefalo animals, and they just didn't perform."

When the Beefalo didn't perform, David and others had formed a breed organization and asked Basolo to have the Beefalo authenticated by blood typing, something Basolo refused to do. Interestingly enough, Burnett had even greater difficulties with Basolo, who took full credit for the development of Beefalo. Burnett confirmed the blood typing question: "He never did blood type any of them, so there's no way of really knowing. He could have traced the parentage to 903. . . ."

After failing with Basolo's Beefalos, David decided to breed his own on the ranch and sent Buddy on a trip to Arkansas, South Dakota, Montana, and Wyoming to track down anyone who might have crossed a buffalo with a cow. As a result, he found other ranchers who were creating hybrids with artificial insemination. The search also led to Burnett, whom David remembers as "a real gentleman." They exchanged visits, and David employed 903's semen, starting his own version of a bison-cattle mix. A picture of 903, a white-faced bull, still hangs at the Selah ranch office.

David, knowing as well as anyone the powers of marketing, combined the name of a popular cattle line called "Beefmaster" with his goal of creating a hybrid that would be a highly efficient grazer, and came up with the name "Grassmaster." As he had with the well-drilling business, David jumped into breeding without knowing anything about it, not even that animal science dictated that his experiment would take years and years. An artificial insemination program was developed, but it proved expensive: the animals had to be kept in top breeding condition, fed well, and closely monitored.

Eventually, David paid for five studies conducted in conjunction with Texas A&M University and Our Lady of the Lake College in San Antonio. This research finally produced positive results: a higher ratio of meat to be cut from the carcass, a more diverse diet, and the ability to digest rougher forms of cellulose. The studies, published in a Grassmaster newsletter, buttressed the breed's credibility in the market. Grassmaster bulls went on display at the San Antonio Stock Show and Rodeo, and there would be seven breeders of Grassmasters and thirty-seven people using Grassmaster bulls on David's bull-loan program. Cattlemen even came from Brazil to learn about the hybrid.

Still, David cited a number of difficulties in marketing the Grass-master: "Convincing people wasn't easy when there are all kinds of cattle breeds. Ranchers are conservative, they are independent, they are opinionated, they are private, and they get hung up on color. They want all white animals or all black animals."

With this in mind, David wanted to develop an appealing, uniform look for his Grassmasters, a particular shade of red. He described what he wanted to Buddy, and Buddy replied, "Well, someone else will have to do it."

"Oh, heck no, we can do it ourselves."

"You don't understand, Dave. That could take a hundred years."

David tried a number of marketing angles, including using his radio station in Austin and his new 1776, Inc. restaurants. He went to the grocery store Whole Foods and offered thousands of dollars worth of radio advertising time if they would put Grassmaster beef in their stores. Whole Foods was tempted but opted out in the end because the Grassmaster meat wasn't consistently available—the herd was too small. The meat was popular—when it was available—at a Fredericksburg market, and the most profitable day for the 1776, Inc. restaurant in San Antonio was the one on which the menu featured Grassmaster chopped steak. Still, the Grassmaster was not a marketing success, although the ranch continued to raise and improve the animal. The program lasted thirty-two years, and David said, "I estimate that the cost over and above what I would have spent if I had just taken a breed of cattle and raised it was a half million dollars. That's gone. I'll never see it."

While neither the Grassmaster nor the Beefalo ended up saving the world, David still believes that his program has genuine merit and has kept the name and the trademark. "The future is going to be the cow that can make a good flavored, quality meat and can graze not just in an irrigated meadow but on hills like we have here."

The Selah family does receive an enviable perk: Grassmaster meat at just the cost of having the animal butchered. Freezers are well stocked. Margaret, David, and I spent a shameful number of evenings on the ranch house patio drinking margaritas and grilling Grassmaster steaks while Margaret and David told fantastical stories.

It was on the patio one evening that David described his scheme to create a beef candy bar to feed the famished in remote parts of the Sahara desert or the mountains of Pakistan and at the same time bolster the Texas beef industry. It was another wild project to save the world, and he is still convinced that, like the Grassmaster, it could work.

David and two friends, Charley Scruggs and Tom Wallace, became partners in the beef candy bar invention. Charley had been the editor of *Southern Living* and vice president in the hierarchy of *The Progressive Farmer*. He was headquartered in Birmingham, Alabama, but bought land relatively near Selah and opened an office in Austin. The other partner, Tom Wallace, had been an executive director of the Texas Sheep and Goat Raisers' Association. David recalled, "Somehow or other, we all came together here on the ranch, just the three of us, no wives, no help. We were brainstorming on what we could do as cattle ranchers to create a product that would have some value to society as a whole and also reward the private landowner ranchers here in Texas. A changing world market and American Heart Association warnings on cholesterol levels and fat content hurt the beef industry. We decided that we could deliver a way of marketing grass-fed beef as opposed to beef coming out of a feedlot. Well, the biggest problem of grass-fed beef is that it's tough. It doesn't have enough fat on it to give it that flavor that you get on a nice, choice steak. We discussed who would eat it and came up with the poor and destitute in places like Africa, Pakistan, and Asia, anywhere people were malnourished. Fat, a waste product in packing plants, could be added as a rich source of calories, which the malnourished need."

The three arrived at the beef candy bar concept and began testing it at Texas A&M University. They figured that theoretically they could drop jerky to the poor from airplanes, but the problem was that even jerky retained moisture and would spoil in only a few weeks. They tried to dry out the beef further, chip it up, and then press it through a large extruder. David explained, "The idea was that you could seal the extruded beef in plastic, and we would fly over the Sahara. We'd drop it out of the airplane. If you want to help a destitute family in the middle of the desert, you drop it. There's no way to deliver it. No refrigeration. Bringing it out to them is totally impossible. You want to be able to drop it from an airplane so that it could be found and used even after three years. We thought about how it could be recognized like a candy bar or a pack of cigarettes. Two things are known all around the planet earth: American cigarettes and candy bars."

The beef candy bar researchers imagined an impoverished man picking up the package, opening it, and chewing on the meat bar or dropping it into a pot of boiling water, but the researchers couldn't perfect the product. Meanwhile, Charley had made some premature press releases, and inquiries were coming from every direction, even the U.N., where Charley spoke of the trio's dream—hatched no doubt over grilled Grassmaster steaks.

Tom, Charley, and David put in $30,000 and raised investments almost twenty times that. They engaged Sterling Foods in San Antonio, a company that provided MRE rations to the military. The company sidetracked the program by unsuccessfully mixing wheat and oats into the beef candy bar. I imagined packets of desiccated meatloaf being dropped into the Sahara. When the 1991 Gulf War started, Sterling Foods turned its attention to providing military food supplies. David is still convinced that the beef candy bar is "a damned good idea."

The Coming of the Scimitar-Horned Oryx

IN THE EARLY 1990s, Emily (Mickey) Hahn wrote a lengthy profile of David for *The New Yorker* and described what would become the Bamberger Ranch Preserve Species Survival Program. At the beginning of the piece, the 85-year-old writer revealed how she had discovered David and his program for the breeding and reintroduction of the critically endangered scimitar-horned oryx:

> We had met by telephone not long after I had seen a segment of
> *60 Minutes* which investigated the auction of surplus zoo animals
> and showed people hunting endangered species on the ranches
> of Texas. It was calculated to arouse the ever-present anger in
> most people opposed to blood sports. Certainly the thought that
> members of endangered species were being butchered for hunters'
> holidays had made me indignant, and I was also curious about
> the presence of these rare animals in Texas. I had telephoned
> several ranchers whose names were given to me by the American
> Association of Zoological Parks and Aquariums. AAZPA mem-
> bers do not sell their animals to game ranches or allow their
> animals to be hunted, but some of the people I called had been
> reluctant to discuss the matter. One had said, cautiously, "You do-
> ing an exposé, or what?" Another had said he wasn't in, but David
> Bamberger, of the Bamberger Ranch, Blanco County, Texas, had
> been willing. . . .

David's twenty-five years of working with the AZA (the contemporary acronym for AAZPA) and contributing to the Species Survival Program

(SSP) amounted to a kind of tragicomedy that mixed controversy, suspicion, inexperience, miscommunication, and negligence. I suspect that the larger story might have at times rankled Hahn. She had come onto the scene only ten years into the captive breeding program at Selah. While David had received local attention for his habitat restoration, Grassmaster program, and environmental activism in helping to create the Guadalupe River State Park, it was Hahn's article in *The New Yorker* that elevated Selah's visibility to a national and international level, generating radio and television interest as well as print coverage. David would admit that he had calculated from the beginning that his involvement with the Species Survival Program would create a platform for him to speak avidly for environmental protection, education, and rehabilitation.

In the late 1970s, David became a board member of the San Antonio Zoo, where he learned that the survival of endangered species was becoming increasingly precarious, with inbreeding in zoos and limited access to genetic diversity. In addition, zoos chronically struggled to work within their budgets and had to cope financially and ethically with surplus animals. Using land donated by private landowners for the protection and controlled revival of an endangered species was a novel concept, and David agreed to dedicate to the SSP approximately one square mile, or 640 acres, of the pastures north and west of Little Mexico. The idea was to centralize genetic material and breeding activity to build up a healthy population and then, if at all possible, reintroduce a particular animal in its original habitat.

From the beginning, David faced suspicion. "I'm waiting four, five, six months. I finally hear that a delegation was coming down." The delegation, comprised of directors of the Bronx, Fort Worth, San Antonio, Denver, Minneapolis, and Henry Doorly Zoos, among others, spent the night at Selah and then inspected and evaluated its resources. "They looked at me, looked at Buddy, looked at Leroy. We showed them the ranch, which looked nothing like it does today. I sold them, but I didn't sell them. They were split about doing something that had never been done before. They asked, 'How can we take animals out of our institutions and put them in the hands of some damned vacuum cleaner peddler or chicken seller or some cowboys here?'" In truth, it was these cowboys who knew something about keeping animals on land and not just locked in cages.

The delegation finally came to an agreement with David. The AZA and the SSP would select the species they felt most suited to Selah's climate conditions and terrain, and they would compute the bloodlines. David, in turn, would dedicate 640 acres of rangeland, including a 50-acre field planted with Kleingrass imported from Africa. He would supply the management along with the required record keeping, in addition to spending $100,000 on construction of alleys, fences, water lines, and the Green Rotunda sifting facility. Leroy went to work immediately, the preparations taking almost a year to complete.

Notice arrived that the SSP had two species of concern: the addax and the scimitar-horned oryx. David recalled, "Hell, I didn't know what either one of them looked like, so I grabbed a book and read about them, then ran down to the San Antonio Zoo to see the actual animals. Over a period of a couple of months, they had decided to do the scimitar-horned oryx because they knew that they had enough genetic material to start the program, and I had pledged that the program would be a model, that I would make it work. Meanwhile, they could use the program to attract other private landowners to become involved."

The agreement stipulated that Selah would not serve as a dumping ground for surplus zoo animals. All animals that came to the ranch would be selected by the SSP on the basis of genetic background. Using computer models to calculate a healthy genetic mix and track bloodlines, the SSP dictated all breeding matches, with the goal of raising the population to four hundred individuals, the number that researchers had decided was necessary to preserve the species over the next 150 years. Finally, all communications passed through a species coordinator specifically assigned to the project. "No one else was supposed to deal with me," David said, "and I wasn't supposed to deal with anyone else."

To receive background on and training in the care of the oryx, David traveled to the National Zoo's Research and Conservation Center, administered by the Smithsonian Institute in Front Royal, Virginia. On arrival, he witnessed the birth of oryx twins, a rare moment David wouldn't experience again. Gregarious and a quick learner, David became well acquainted with the personnel and facilities at the National Zoo as he studied the characteristics of the species.

Back in Texas, David received the very call the SSP had promised that he wouldn't get. A driver called from Austin. "Mr. Bamberger, I'm trying to find you. I got three animals here."

"What?"

"Yeah, three animals."

"What kind do you have?"

"They're oryx."

"Where did they come from?"

"I picked them up in Front Royal, Virginia, up there in Washington."

"Who told you to bring them here?"

"I don't know."

"Well you come out highway 290 and you hit the 281 intersection. I'll meet you there at 2 P.M."

The ranch wasn't prepared for the animals; there was not even fencing. Leroy and Randy quickly tacked together plywood sheets to build a twelve-foot square enclosure with an eight-foot-high solid wall. David called the coordinator. "I've got three scimitar horns from Front Royal. Yeah, three scimitar horns arrived today. I didn't get any paperwork on them."

"Well, you didn't get any paperwork because you weren't supposed to get the animals."

The zoo community had started off on the wrong foot. The three animals were surplus, with no value whatsoever to the SSP program. They had been a burden on the National Zoo, and when zoo officials learned that David had reserved 640 acres to save the species, they perhaps understandably shipped off the animals so they wouldn't have to feed them. In addition, the Bamberger Ranch had signed a contract stating that the animals wouldn't be shot or sold to exotic hunting ranches.

Despite the problematic qualities of the three oryx, the Selah team quickly learned important lessons in handling captive animals. Putting the oryx inside the makeshift enclosure ironically turned out to be one of the smartest things they could do, as they would learn later when an oryx arrived from Detroit. The fences were in place by then, and after the trailer pulled into the pasture and the gate was opened, the animal shot out, running a quarter of a mile at full speed, hit the fencing, and trampolined backward. It was the first time the animal's feet had touched dirt and grass out in the open. From then on, every time Leroy and Randy received an animal, it was quarantined in the box. David claimed, "We probably saved a half-dozen animals from breaking their necks."

The program began in earnest. The SSP and AZA researched records and traced thirty-three oryx that had been extirpated from Africa and found that twenty-nine of them, representing thirty-one bloodlines, were still alive. It took two years to bring twenty-four oryx to Selah. Those animals carried twenty-nine of the thirty-one bloodlines for which scrupulous records would be maintained. The SSP director, who was also monitoring the addax program, was able to weed out populations that had redundant genetic material since any number of animals at a given zoo may be descendants of the same sire.

The program was functioning well until an eleven-inch snowstorm carpeted Blanco County, the cold and the snow lingering for the good part of a week. Two of the oryx, vulnerable in frigid weather, froze to death. David recalled, "It was like picking up statues." Leroy quickly installed an incubator system, and the ranch never lost another animal to cold weather. However, the loss of two animals was a disappointment to the Selah team and the zoo community, some of whom were surely muttering, "I told you these cowboys couldn't do this." Still, the breeding program prospered, and scientists and researchers were sent from various universities to draw blood, analyze the genetics, and initiate studies. When animals were born, they were tattooed with numbers registered in the International Species Identification Program. A report on the parents was matched with the computer models, and the tags were placed in the left or right ear, depending on the animal's sex.

Despite the apparent success of the program, many in the zoo community continued to distrust the Texas ranchers, believing that only trained specialists could handle such a critical operation. In addition, Selah maintained a hunting program, which was antithetical to AZA principles and to the spirit of animal rights, a growing movement at the time. When the national convention of AZA was held in Dallas in the mid-1980s, a post-convention tour of the Bamberger Ranch was arranged for an inspection of the breeding program. The AZA chartered four buses to transport two hundred convention participants to Selah.

"Some of those people knew just damn well that we had screwed up. They were going to catch us red-handed," David recalled. The participants toured Texas exotic ranches prior to their eventual arrival at Selah. "If you are from Chicago or New York City and you are on a big tour down here, every ranch you come to will serve you barbecue. It's just Texas. I had some moxie. I called my engineers and said, 'Look. I want a Church's Fried Chicken store on my ranch.' They went to work, and right beside Hes' Country Store they built a Church's Fried Chicken."

The engineers installed a level platform floor and moved in three fryers, a batter table, and a counter. The configuration was identical to that of a commercial store. Cooks could fry thirty chickens at a time, four two-piece orders to a bird. It took seven minutes to prepare the chicken and twenty-one minutes to fry it. A sequential rotation was set up for the three fryers so that the orders were always freshly cooked.

Selah was blessed with a balmy day for the visit. As soon as the buses showed up at the gate, David got the call and then gave the order, "Boys, throw the chicken." By the time buses had passed the grave for mankind at Malabar and the water crossings in Pleasant Valley, and then made their way up between Windsong and High Lonesome, the famished visitors disembarked from the bus into the gratifying aroma of frying chicken. David said, "Well, when you've got brand-new shortening, brand new flour, the shortening is up to 340 degrees, and you throw that chicken in, it's like when you go into a bakery, your baker is baking bread, oh that delicious smell. Where else are you going to find a fried chicken store out in the middle of a ranch with a population of four?" In addition, French fries, jalapeños, and soft drinks were offered as if the visitors had walked into a store in San Antonio. The group flocked from the buses over to the unlikely fried chicken store set in a meadow, the only other building being a shack with deer antlers and a cigar store Indian out front. Everybody sat down and ate and then ate some more, grateful for something besides barbecue. After lunch, they looked at the country store or walked part of the Bromfield Trail along the creek.

David had set a festive stage before the viewing of the oryx. The scientists, biologists, and zoo managers, accoutered with binoculars and scratch pads (to itemize the ranch's deficiencies, no doubt) boarded the Selah red and blue trailers, with bales of hay for seats. Randy and Leroy drove the group out to "The Sahara," where, almost as in a dream, a herd of seventy scimitar-horned oryx grazed on pastureland, a sight impossible anywhere else in the world, something long lost in Sudan, Chad, Niger, and Libya. The males, as always, were pastured separately. Every animal sported an ear tag, and none showed the scratches, cuts, and rubbing often seen on zoo animals that battle each other or harm themselves out of boredom.

David is forever on the offensive against "the PhDs," as he calls them, the tribe who may be gifted academic lecturers and writers but who are in his estimation incapable of applying the most fundamental elements of common sense. Of course, David isn't alone in attacking scientists. Anti-intellectualism has long been a crowd-pleasing American pastime.

Randy fielded questions. "How do you manage to file their hooves?"

"I do that every day."

"That's impossible," the incredulous scientist responded, knowing that the zoo has to employ anesthesia on each occasion of filing hooves.

"I just let them do it themselves running around in the field."

David said to me, "The PhD with a suit should know this. Now that's not rocket science. I get a call from a guy in New York who read in the literature on our program. 'I want to thank you personally, Mr. Bamberger. This is something we've needed for a long time. When you have your 2,000 animals, I want to come down and see them.' I said, 'Doctor, I appreciate your calling me and your positive attitude, but I'm never going to have 2,000 animals.' 'What about the 640 acres you've given us for this program?' 'Yes sir, but 640 acres can only carry eighty-eight animals.' The guy tells me his zoo is only 18 acres and they have a 2,200 animal collection. I said, 'Well, sir, how much of a feed bill do you have?' He said $800,000 a year.' I said, 'Sir, how many veterinarians do you have?' 'We have three, full-time.' 'Well, our feed bill will probably be more like $800, and we have no veterinarians. I'm not going to destroy years of restoration work by overgrazing. We will carry only the herd that Mother Nature can provide for.'"

The next year David was invited to speak at the AZA convention, with twelve hundred participants, in Ft. Lauderdale, Florida. He scolded his audience: "By God, you may be good scientists, but you are piss-poor businessmen." For better or worse, going against the grain was now a Bamberger tradition, whether in fighting for environmental legislation or in dealing with zoologists, ecologists, and animal rights activists.

International interest in the oryx survival program continued to grow, prompting participation from places as disparate as Cuba, Canada, and Egypt. David received a letter from Dr. Morino, director of the Havana Zoo, explaining that he had read about Selah's work and had something very valuable to offer the program. In the 1970s, when Muammar al-Khadafy invaded Chad, Libyan soldiers discovered and captured a rare group of scimitar-horned oryx in the wild, and a pair was sent as a gift to Castro's national zoo. Clearly, the fresh genetic material would provide a boost to Selah's program, and David responded enthusiastically. Repeated missives received no response. Deducing finally that his letters were being blocked, David took the problem to an SSP coordinator, who arranged the shipment of an offspring of the Havana pair to the Toronto Zoo. There, the animal had to be quarantined. David sent his own animal to the Henry Doorly Zoo in Nebraska, which sent it on to Canada. The animal was bred so that half of the new genetic pool could be pulled into the Selah program. Another scimitar-horned oryx was discovered in a zoo in Cairo and shipped to San Diego, where it was quarantined, then mistakenly delivered to Denver for a couple of years before arriving at the ranch.

David, under the auspices of the (then) World Wildlife Fund, visited Niger to assess the feasibility of reintroducing the oryx. The expedition, with area experts and military escort, would take him to the Gadabeji Reserve. Along the way, in places like Agadez, David would experience extremes of human desperation, which he recorded in his personal journal. The journal entries reveal a gradual shift from his habitual optimism to insuperable doubt. David wrote,

> We're moving closer to oryx country. My first impressions are favorable. Gentle rolling grassland with scattered trees. No oryx spotted here since the late 60s. Savannah now, lots of dead trees from the 60s and 70s drought. Seeing more people, many more cattle, especially near the wells. I don't see how they can survive. I'm told that they drive cattle to water every other day and they keep reaching out farther from the wells for grass.

By the time he reached the Gadabeji Reserve, David had been sick for several days, and members of the expedition grew disgruntled with difficult travel. David appreciated the potential of the land but bemoaned its condition. He wrote,

> There are too many cattle. Even the camels are thin. The dust is getting thicker, visibility just a quarter mile. We spot some eagles swooping in on a rabbit. Five more red-fronted gazelles. They

are larger than the dorcas gazelles. This could be a beautiful place. Rolling plains, scattered trees. It just needs a long rest for revegetation.

David gained distance on the novelty of his expedition, although he appreciated meeting and traveling with John Newby, the International Union for the Conservation of Nature representative for all of Africa, and other engaged experts, and also the workshops in Niamey, Niger's capitol. In the *New Yorker* profile, he told Hahn of the oryx, "The country isn't fit for them. It's too poor—everyone is poor. It was clear that my oryx wouldn't survive there." Who would argue against a man feeding his starving family at the expense of an endangered animal? David, in his journal, viewed himself through the eyes of others. "With so many problems here, why worry about our animals? I believe our drivers and guides think we are nuts!"

David would go to Niger again to evaluate a fenced area next to a newly constructed housing community. It was a French attempt to build a compound, but when locals moved in, they built their fires tradition-ally on the living room floors. Blown sand simply accumulated against the fences. David was ready to commit a year of his life to preparing an environment for Selah's oryx, the extremes of Africa haunting him. But the site was not even remotely adequate.

Meanwhile, by the 1990s much had changed in the zoo community. While zoos themselves had improved their own breeding programs and some of the conditions under which animals were kept, the com-munity still struggled financially, and an administrative changing-of-the-guard took place. David said that most new administrators and zoo personnel were avid animal rights people who continued to raise objections to Selah's hunting program and harbor suspicions that the oryx were hunted on the ranch. At the same time, zoo programs were forced to make cutbacks. David soon found communication increas-ingly difficult, despite the tremendous media attention he had received for the program.

David had forty-five animals that were five years old or older and had never been bred. He alerted the SSP. The animals had to be bred, or their ability to reproduce would be severely compromised simply by aging. The stock of genetic material was at risk. The SSP responded that this was not true. David told me, "Well I pissed them off. There's an association of zoo veterinarians. The highest level of achievement you could get as a veterinarian was the rank of diplomat. There were only thirty-nine at the time in the U.S., and I contacted five of them, asking 'Do you think it will hurt to let young scimitar-horned oryx females reach five and six years old without ever breeding them? Would this affect future breeding?' Four out of the five of the veterinary diplomats said, 'You bet it would.' This pissed off the PhDs because they already said, no, it won't. So I don't make any friends with that one."

The coordinator finally gave the order to breed all forty-five at once and provided a pairing scheme based on the computer selections. The Selah team went to work, only to suffer the most distressing results in the whole history of the program—miscarriages, abandoned calves, and two females dying while birthing. David remains bitter over the SSP's handling of the program. "I'm no scientist. Leroy has been around animals his entire life. Buddy knows cows. It doesn't matter whether they are cows, dogs, or oryx. It's just plain sense that there's a time for breeding."

Tensions only increased, and the critical point of contention was David's conviction that hunting ranches served a highly practical purpose. "The biggest problem in all zoos in the United States is surplus. They don't know what to do with extra animals, and they don't have the space for them. There's only one thing to do. Euthanize them. I was told that 50% of animals born in the San Antonio Zoo are euthanized using the time of veterinarians and chemicals. It's not only terrible, but I can sell every one of them and bring in thousands of much needed dollars for conservation. The zoos are on their knees begging for money. Who would buy these animals? David Bamberger and his neighbors and Hill Country ranchers who run hunting operations to make a living, but the PETA people and the board of directors of the AZA said absolutely not."

Although prohibited in many states, hunting ranches have an incentive to preserve a particular exotic species: their business depends on it. Ike C. Sugg, former executive director of the Exotic Wildlife Association, underlined David's argument in a *Wall Street Journal* article just a year after *The New Yorker* profile:

> As Mr. Bamberger laments, "altruism will not save the species." If game ranchers lose interest in a species, its future is imperiled. Those with an economic stake in a natural resource have every reason to maximize that which is valuable, which means increasing wildlife numbers. It means preserving the genetic purity of the species, from which its value is often derived. And it means taking care of the land—a collateral ecological benefit.

Twenty years after the oryx program was started, David and Margaret flew out to Arizona to report to the regional meetings of the antelope studbook keepers and the SSP committees. David presented his slide show of the oryx program along with data backing years of positive results achieved at Selah. Some of the PhDs faulted the program for not being sufficiently scientific, even though the Selah team had followed to the letter what the SSP had told them to do. According to David, the committee charged that the selection should have been made more carefully, under stricter controls, and there should have been an equal ratio of males to females. The conclusion was that none of his animals now qualified for the Species Survival Program.

David asked, "What can I do with them? They told me I could euthanize them. I don't have the chemicals, and I don't have the veterinarian. 'Well you can use a 30.06.' That's a deer rifle. Think about this," David said, still fuming after four years. "I can't sell the animal for $5,000 to a hunting ranch and let them euthanize him. But I can euthanize it and bury the damn carcass. And I can euthanize it with a gun. That is so asinine to me. I look at that application that costs me $500 a year to be a member. I had been a member for seventeen years already. Now they want to know what my crisis management plan is. They want to know how many people visit my institution a year and what my gate receipts amount to. I put in 'not applicable' again and again. They said that this is not an acceptable application. Well, I tore it up and took the forty-five animals they didn't want, and I start selling them to hunting ranches. You know why the hunting ranches are dying for them? It's because the ones they have are inbred to the extent that they are malformed, dwarfs, or even albino. One of them was an albino with pink eyes." David made $37,000 that year selling scimitar-horned oryx, the first income Selah had ever received from them. Burkhard Bilger, writing again on the oryx for *The New Yorker*, almost exactly ten years after Hahn, explained also that the meat from hunting ranches is often given to the poor:

> . . . . they (the hunters) aren't really interested in the meat. They want the serendipity of a good hunt without its incertitude, and when they're done all they need is the trophy head to remember it by. Every year, the ranch gives away five thousand pounds of unclaimed meat to groups like Hunters for the Hungry.

While Margaret was in serious condition and my wife, Mary, was staying at the ranch and making the trip each morning to the Fredericksburg hospital, a zoo delegation from California, Front Royal, and Cincinnati arrived at Selah and stayed the night. David warned them that he might have to leave at any moment for the hospital. The delegation had come to ask David to rejuvenate the breeding program in order to reintroduce the oryx in North Africa. For the first time, they had proposed to David a plausible strategy, and they recognized that they couldn't achieve their goal without his participation.

David said to me, "For the next few years, we're not going to have many animals to sell. I am producing animals that are going to go to Gambia, Morocco, Senegal, perhaps Israel, and some to Tunisia." The delegation had proposed these countries as potential sites. David assured me that the scimitar-horned oryx will continue to be a part of the Selah

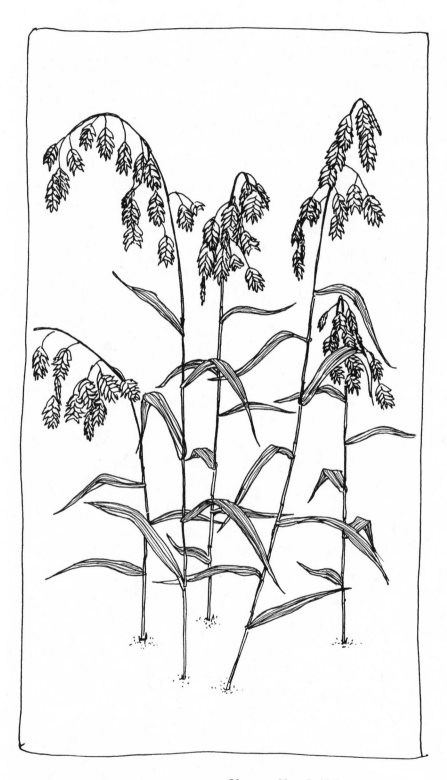

BROADLEAF WOODOATS *Chasmanthium latifolium*

Species Survival Program, even after he is gone. In addition to supplying animals for reintroduction into Africa, Selah will ship an animal for free, anywhere in the world where there is a good genetic match and interest in participating in the breeding program.

"What provoked the change of heart?" I asked.

"They had to face the reality. They couldn't do it in their institutions. They didn't have the space, and they didn't have the money to move the animals around. Every bit of this is the God-awful truth."

The Center

THE CENTER IS a symmetrical building with a boys' dormitory on the left and a girls' dormitory on the right, a division of gender that reminds me of old grammar school entrances, although the atmosphere of the building is entirely contemporary. The middle provides a multi-purpose space: conference room, schoolroom, library, nature display area, and cafeteria with restaurant-quality cooking facilities equipped to accommodate large numbers of guests. An enormous fireplace dominates the middle of the common space, and on it are mounted heads of a water buffalo, an American Bison, two caribou, and a scimitar-horned oryx. Most of the heads came from the San Antonio Zoo, which decided to relegate them to storage. David, on the zoo board at the time, was delighted to take the heads off their hands, so to speak.

The Mexicans laid the base stonework for the building, the porch flooring, and patio with arbor shading. The interior walls are paneled with pine, and spacious ceilings draw off heat. Blue banners with white lettering—inspirational passages on the environment—hang from a major crossbeam. David began to see the symmetry of the building as a symbol.

In private conversation, David was outraged by governmental policies that led directly to environmental damage, military aggression, deteriorating infrastructure, and the alienation of Cuba. He even questioned the strength of American democracy, with its cronyism, powerful special interests, and gerrymandered voting districts. However, he also understood the efficacy of finding common ground. Certainly, managing a vacuum cleaner sales force took *savoir-faire*, and social dexterity was required for speaking on Wall Street one day and setting up a fried chicken store in some forsaken neighborhood the next. Above all, and where it counted most, David recognized that any initiative for effective environmental rehabilitation and legislation had to engage both the political left and right.

When David had The Center built, he envisioned a place for enlightened debate, a common ground from which productive environmental activism could be launched despite broad social, political, and religious differences. In reflections called "Restoring Place," he described The Center's symbolic nature:

> The Center was named after a great deal of prayer and thought. It's named that way because I wanted to bring people from as far on one side of the issue as the other. My goal was to get all those people who are thinking on conservation issues to come together. It's the center where most things are made to happen. It's the eye of the hurricane, the center, where the most calm is. It's the center of the aisle where political deals are struck.

The 1980s were in many ways the most turbulent years in David's life, starting with Hes' death on May 15, 1980, followed by the leveraged buyout of Church's Fried Chicken, and finally the painful deterioration of his marriage of forty-five years. It was also a decade in which he began to solidify the Selah programs and his environmental philosophy. Around the time The Center was built, David was enlisted to reorganize the company leadership. Church's Fried Chicken had grown less productive, with the unhappy pairing of an overpaid CEO and a far more competitive market. Speaking to Wall Street analysts in 1983 and introducing a new management team, David outlined his role on coming back to Church's as the chairman of the board:

> As you people well know, there's a new environment out there—a Bamberger statistic says that forty out of fifty new restaurants built in America today are unneeded. So what that said to me

was that I had to do the thing I knew best: use my common sense and people skills—which are standard ingredients for success—lay ego aside, and put together a new management group.

The environment had changed more than David had anticipated, and he was introducing the handpicked team who would in the end betray him and the company. He often said to me, "It was my own damn fault. I hired them." But a new climate had taken hold among high-energy American business executives more attuned to corporate power moves than to fostering a company through the careful production, attractive incentives, and friendships of the old school. As for hobnobbing in a boardroom with other execs, David would prefer paving a muddy parking lot with cardboard boxes to open a new Church's store. He loved building stores, not to mention relationships with the crews he hired, and he based his business philosophy on what he had learned in the tiresome and tough world of vacuum cleaner sales: provide clear incentives. It was a principle he would advocate later for bridging the interests of private landowners and those of endangered species.

David's antics on Wall Street continued when speaking during an investment conference. An analyst who followed the restaurant industry questioned him on how Church's could compete against the thirty-five million dollar marketing plans of Kentucky Fried Chicken. "What is your plan and how much do you plan to spend?" the analyst asked. David responded that Church's plans called for spending a few hundred thousand dollars and was summed up in two sentences, but he doubted the analyst would understand. "The customers who come have to get more for their money than a box of fried chicken. Employees have to get more for their work than a paycheck."

David had been particularly proud of a deal he'd struck with Sam Walton. It occurred to David to set up mini-versions of his stores on Wal-Mart parking lots. To get Walton's attention, David sent his two Lear jet pilots to Wal-Mart's Arkansas headquarters with a proposal: 4% of store sales for the location rights for each Church's. Delighted with the idea, Walton called David and proposed a trial involving three restaurants. They were unequivocal successes, and nine more sites were planned. The new Church's executives, including the CEO David had recruited, asked: Why give Wal-Mart 4% when Church's could build on adjacent land and simply profit by proximity?

Sitting with me, David suffered visibly at the memory, even sixteen years later. Donna remembered the treacherous atmosphere of those days, having intuited the conspiratorial nature of the execs coming out to Selah. She even thought there had been an attempt to bug the ranch house. A degree of paranoia was unquestionably warranted. Worst of all, the marriage became deeply strained.

David characterized the executives as Ivy League PhDs and MBAs. "They got the idea to do a leveraged buyout. It wasn't enough for them to control the company. Those guys got dollar signs in their eyes." The main buyout strategy was revealed with a "tombstone ad" placed in the *Wall Street Journal* and other major newspapers, stating that twenty million shares would be bought on a first-come, first-served basis at two dollars over the market value. As an officer and major shareholder, David could not deal in his own securities without violating insider-trading statutes. Those involved in the buyout would incur a huge debt, which they planned to cover by liquidating some of Church's real estate assets and then signing leases. However, the stores were built in some of the worst neighborhoods, where land values were low. Problems were exacerbated when a deep recession hit Texas. Banks were folding, and the real estate market tumbled. The buyout progressed gradually while the stock dropped from $35 a share to $9 before recovering some. The official takeover was complete when Popeye's "whipped" Church's in 1989.

Ralph Kovel said, "I remember when he got out of Church's. David said it was the worst day of his life. It wasn't losing the money that hurt. He just lost control of the company, and it became someone else's business." The crowning blow was Donna's request for a divorce. David moved out, setting up an office and living quarters in a development he was constructing with his son on the north side of San Antonio. He would flourish as an entrepreneur with his Entre Nous Enterprises. More importantly, looking to rebuild his life, he focused more fully on Selah's programs and other work for environmental causes.

In the late 1980s, David, now both notorious and celebrated for his land stewardship and conservation efforts, received a call from Andy Sansom, a handsome environmentalist in his late thirties, executive director of the Texas Nature Conservancy. He wanted to enlist David in Texas state conservation efforts. As David recalled it, "Andy says, 'Mr. Bamberger, I want to show you something really unique. I'd like to take you out to Bracken Cave. You are welcome to bring your family along.' 'Andy, I'll tell you what, I'll not only bring my grandchildren and my son, but I'll also bring two big family boxes of Church's chicken, and we'll just eat out there.' So he takes me out to Bracken Cave. You have to crawl to get in there. It takes forty minutes to go from the gate to the cave. It is so thick with cedar you struggle. We ate that chicken, drank some Coke. All of a sudden, those bats come out of there. Honest to God, it's the eighth wonder of the world. Unbelievable! From that moment on, I'm a convicted bat enthusiast." It turned out that he had just seen, according to Tuttle's *Texas Bats,* "the world's largest community of mammals": twenty million, mostly female, Mexican free-tailed bats.

The connection with Andy Sansom turned out to be timely, as a deep despondency had seized David after leaving Donna. He sought a productive way to rebuild his life and revive his passions. The organization called Bat Conservation International and the members of the Texas Parks and Wildlife Department provided the community he had hoped for. He donated $10,000 to the combined efforts of BCI and the Texas Nature Conservancy in developing the Eckert James River Bat Cave site, efforts which mainly involved building trails and providing signage.

Andy Sansom had changed positions, first working for the real estate section of Texas Parks and Wildlife, then moving up to the department's executive directorship. By this time, Emily Hahn's profile of David had appeared in *The New Yorker* and had ignited both local and national media interest in Selah. Andy called David, proposing a two-day seminar at The Center for his staff and inviting Governor Ann Richards as keynote speaker. Of course, David couldn't have been more delighted, and he and the governor quickly established a rapport. "I'm there as the host and Andy introduces me to the governor," David remembered. "I charm her, and she charms me a little bit. I present her with a jar of Bamberger Ranch honey. About a week later, I get a little card from her. 'Boy, that honey sure was sweet, and it was sweet of you to give it to me.' Another month passes, and Andy calls, saying, 'The governor wants to meet you.' I asked, 'Is she married?' After my first couple of times being with her, I get a call from the appointments secretary for the governor. 'We have an opening for chairman for the International Trade Commission. The governor wanted me to ask if you would be interested in being chairman.' 'I don't know a goddamn thing about international trade, but I'll take it,' I told them. That began the connection. She appoints me to the Task Force on Nature Tourism in Texas. Then I become an ex-officio member of the Texas Department of Commerce Policy Board."

David and the governor developed a deep respect for each other, and both benefited from their association. They socialized, taking a five-day group trip together canoeing down the Rio Grande, with guitar-playing and good food. David had ambitions for a six-year appointment to the Texas Parks and Wild Life Department Commission, but that dream was put to an abrupt end with George W. Bush's solid defeat of Richards, his insertion of his own officials, and his slashing of state support for many environmental initiatives. Through the years, Ann Richards, along with Andy Sansom and Lady Bird Johnson, remained a keen supporter of Selah.

In 1988 David had already become a trustee of the San Antonio Zoo; in 1992 he was appointed a trustee for Bat Conservation International, serving also as the chairman of Bracken Cave. While he served on the governor's Task Force on Nature Tourism in Texas, his ideas began to coalesce. From his early years at Selah, he had been concerned about how ranchers could survive in a delicate ecosystem that was never really suited to raising stock, thus the history of devastation of the land and the heartbreaking ranch failures that are so much a part of the Hill Country lore. Private landowners' ability to provide hunting and fishing leases generated some income opportunities and incentives to maintain quality conditions for attractive game. But David began to understand the huge revenue potential in nature tourism, and more complex ecosystems would support an even greater variety of flora and fauna—birds in particular, as well as wildflowers and butterflies. He went a step further, arguing that the presence of endangered species, the sheer novelty of their appearing on a ranch, was quite a valuable commodity in itself. The number of birdwatchers who would come to Selah just to see a golden-cheeked warbler or a black-capped vireo was telling evidence. The environmental movement engendered interest in nature tourism, or "ecotourism," a growing international industry that could benefit ranchers, tourists, and the natural world itself.

The income was obvious, to David's thinking, but he was straying once again into extremely controversial territory. Most Americans supported legislation protecting endangered species, leading Congress to pass the Endangered Species Conservation Act, which through amendments became more defined in its language, covering international trade in endangered species and broadening the powers of federal and state agencies to acquire land and impose regulations on private landowners. In Texas, private landowners, and ranchers in particular, saw the Endangered Species Act as a license for government infringement on the sacred freedom to conduct business and manage property as the owner considered fit. Under the law, the Sierra Club and other advocacy groups could file suit against development, mining, oil drilling, logging, and the like in the name of protecting a certain endangered fish, frog, salamander, or bird. When the Endangered Species Act was reviewed for reauthorization, a congressional task force was assembled and sent around the country to gather information. It held a hearing at the Kendall

County Fairgrounds in an incendiary atmosphere, as described by Roy Bragg in the *San Antonio Express-News:*

> The Beltway came to the Hill Country on Monday and the result was tent-revival fervor, as professional politicians and farmers preached for change in the Endangered Species Act.
>
> About 750 people squeezed into the Kendall County Fairgrounds meeting hall to hear flaming rhetoric about a law they view as unfair, largely unnecessary, and detrimental to farming.

One rancher, referring to a Sierra Club lawsuit in favor of protecting the fountain darter, said, "It's just a socialistic maneuver to take over private property." The few environmentalists attending the hearing remained silent. David, who was asked to testify, proved to be the only private rancher who spoke in favor of the act, in the face of resounding boos. Unfazed, he delivered his prepared statement, conceding that the act had flaws and criticizing the government for "force feeding" legislation rather than educating the public and raising its awareness. However, he asked the committee to provide leadership to America by re-authorizing the Endangered Species Act. They would be telling the country that endangered species were important, and the people would respond. David's central message was that protecting endangered species, which collaterally meant protecting healthy ecosystems, is profitable. In his testimony to Congress, he gave two examples:

> I am aware of a ranch right here in the Hill Country that brought two groups to their ranch and earned $14,000 just for the bird watching. And the primary reason that these two groups came to that ranch was to see the endangered golden-cheeked warbler and the endangered black-capped vireo.
>
> In 1993, gentlemen and ladies, up here on Lake LBJ, which is about 30 miles from my ranch, there's a boat dock sticking out on the water and some little bird got blown off course from

its Pacific flyway. It's called the blue-footed booby. Today he's in one of our state parks. That little bird's navigational system got knocked out and he landed up there on that boat dock and stayed six months. And let me tell you it's estimated that a quarter of a million dollars was spent by people coming from Connecticut and Florida and Missouri and Ohio, all over the nation, just to look at that little bird and write his name down in their little lifetime book.

David looked at the whole spectrum of economic benefits to a rural community from ecotourism: its impact on car rentals, hotels, restaurants, gas stations, small town shops, and so forth. His fellow landowners clearly and vehemently saw the act as an infringement on their rights, but David was content to be perhaps the only rancher in the state to defend its renewal. As reported by *The Dallas Morning News:* "he has no regrets, finding satisfaction in making 'a contribution to the whole state of Texas and to wildlife.'" David's stand did not go unappreciated. He received a laudatory letter from Todd H. Votteler, a Sierra Club administrator, stating, "I want to tell you that I admire you for standing up for a law that, while not perfect, has accomplished a great deal. Yours was the lone voice of reason among a sea of fear and anger."

David was also involved in getting Proposition 11 approved in 1995. This state constitutional amendment extended the agricultural tax exemption for ranchers; it would now also apply when livestock and crop activities were redirected to wildlife management. The Texas property tax code requires that the land must have been of primarily agricultural use for a minimum of "five of seven preceding years" and defines wildlife management as activity meeting at least three of seven criteria intended to propagate and sustain the "breeding, migrating, or wintering population of indigenous wild animals for human use, including food, medicine, or recreation." The seven criteria are "habitat control, erosion control, predator control, providing supplemental supplies of water, providing supplemental supplies of food, providing shelters, and making census counts to determine population."

Directly southwest of The Center in the area called Guzzler Loop, an open hilltop with a 360-degree view of Selah and beyond, David constructed a wildlife management demonstration area protected by fencing that kept out cows but not deer and other animals. It's one of my favorite spots on the ranch because it feels wide open to the elements and the sky—to wind, stars, and sunsets. Invariably, wild turkeys, deer, jackrabbits, fox, or armadillos are rustling about. The demonstration area features different provisions and devices that directly address the criteria for a wildlife management tax exemption.

The first device you come to is a rather ominous walk-in-size steel cage that serves as a cowbird trap. The brown-headed bird with a black body unfortunately lays its eggs in the nests of up to two hundred and twenty other species. With a short gestation period, and instinctually aggressive, the cowbird young easily displace other hatchlings and so have become a major threat to songbirds, including the rare golden-cheeked warbler and the other Hill Country avian specialty, the black-capped vireo. Before the pioneers arrived, the cowbirds followed the migratory bison—switching later to cattle herds—feeding on insects. Today, with songbird populations threatened, cowbirds often have to be trapped and killed (by cervical dislocation) to keep their numbers in check.

Entering the demonstration area, you come to the v-shaped panels of the rain-capturing guzzler, with cistern and watering pool. Behind it, an outdoor classroom is arranged in a semicircle under the shade of oaks and facing a series of boxes that illustrate proper housing for bluebirds, ducks, owls, and bats. Nearby, oats, rye, alfalfa, and turnips grow along with other tubers and sedges for deer, and a collection of shrubs attracts birds and butterflies, all forming a miniature plot to show how to provide supplemental food, water, and shelter for wildlife.

The last time I'd been up at Guzzler Loop was for a Stewardship Workshop taught by Steven Fulton and Scott Grode. Steven, twenty-six, a 6' 8" nature boy, was raised in Rosebud, Texas, with three brothers and three sisters, a family conspicuously large in size as well as number.

A bright, observant kid, though reserved, somewhat of a social outcast in school, he learned the local bird songs and could imitate them. He absorbed the names of wildflowers, grasses, shrubs, and trees, as well as Texas geology, so that it was easy for him to move into the role of a Selah educator. Meanwhile, Scott took over both Buddy's spot as the cow Aggie and Randy's as deer Aggie. The strong impression I got from Scott and Steven—and from Leroy, for that matter—is that if required to, they could walk off into the hills with nothing but a knife and be able to survive off the land with as much facility, if none of the grandstanding feats or Native American mysticism, as Eustace Conaway, famed subject of *The Last American Man.* They have an uncanny connection to the land, the natural world, much as Bromfield's Max Drake did.

For most of the workshop, Steven talked and Scott drove the trailer, except when both extolled the healing powers of prescribed burns and showed off the quality of grasses that returned in the place of greenbrier and cactus after they'd used a drip torch on whole fields. They were so enthusiastic that I thought they might well go on to recommend napalm. David wasn't thrilled with the burnt look but understood its necessity. When we reached Guzzler Loop, wild turkeys clucked in the brush, buzzards cruised overhead, and black butterflies floated by. Several participants were clearly keen to learn more about the wildlife tax exemption. In particular, a woman with only sixteen acres was interrogating Scott, who stood looking his cowboy best, in Stetson and reflective sunglasses, in front of an owl house. "How do I get a wildlife exemption?"

Steven simply knelt, quietly bowed his head, and started pulling on some grass. Scott, speaking up, strained to be diplomatic, knowing that beating the system was the woman's primary interest, but his integrity got the better of him. He explained, "First you have to have an agricultural exemption, and then you can switch if you meet the criteria."

"Well, how do I get an agricultural exemption? How many animals? How much land do I need to clear?"

"You have sixteen acres? Well, you go to your county tax assessor, and he'll say that's not enough acreage to run one cow. Or they may come to your place and see three or four goats and ask if it's truly helpful for everyone else to give you this tax break on your small acreage."

"A guy in our town got one on ten acres," another participant offered.

"It depends on a number of factors, and it is not enough just to be classified as agricultural land. We're into conservation here, and stewardship. Do you really want to see someone run four cows on seven acres? It doesn't work from a conservation standpoint. They might in certain cases get it pushed through, but is that a good thing? I know everyone would like an exemption. But the spirit of the thing was for production of agriculture, something that benefits everybody, something that's providing food for other people. For wildlife too, it has to benefit everybody else. Now if you are truly providing a habitat that's helping some endangered species or something like that, you may have a real good shot."

Scott went on to explain the complexities of providing for wildlife, that difficult balances must be maintained in deer populations because they threaten endangered plant species, not to mention food sources for other animals. Likewise, rampant raccoon populations endanger ground-nesting birds, such as the quail, which has become ever more scarce in the Hill Country. Scott argued that we are now responsible for restoring what our predecessors have thrown out of whack in nature.

The issue of beating taxes fell by the wayside, but Scott's telling the group to pay attention to the original spirit of the legislation, that the exemptions were put into place as an incentive to provide a benefit for all, has continued to resonate in me. The spirit he urged was in accord with values that David had formulated in the early 1990s for environmental advocacy, some of which remind me of Kennedy's famous words, with a twist: "Ask not what Mother Nature can do for you. Ask what you can do for Mother Nature."

At the top of David's concerns was that the more squeezed by urban growth natural habitats become, the more they will be accessible only to an elite. This phenomenon makes itself particularly evident on privately owned shorelines, and lovers of the natural world can learn all too quickly how high the entrance fees have become at Texas parks. As David received invitations to speak around the country, he emphasized ten steps that should be taken to enhance our relationship with nature:

1. We should make parks accessible to all, especially members of lower socio-economic groups.

2. We should tell our legislators that we want public funding for our parks just as we do for education, highways, fire protection, and police.

3. We should set aside more land for refuges, parks, and natural areas.

4. To make outdoor experiences available to the public and to give some financial benefits to private landowners, a system of "Franchise Parks" should be developed by park and wildlife departments.

5. Every child in the first grade and every year thereafter should be assigned an organism—a bug, plant, animal, or tree—to study and report on.

6. All college students in agriculture, conservation, and environmental studies should, as part of their degree requirements, spend one year as an intern on a farm or ranch, doing all the chores associated with such an operation.

7. We should "incentivize" the protection of endangered species by offering substantial cash rewards to private landowners who propagate, nurture, and protect plant and animal species endangered or threatened with extinction.

8. We should agree upon long-range land-use plans, and society should equitably compensate private landowners whose land values may be adversely affected by such plans.

9. We should enlist the talents of screen- and script writers so that environmental concerns and conservation principles are woven into educational programs, movies, and other media.

10. We should recognize and reward the organizations and the individuals who volunteer their time and energy on behalf of the natural world.

For years, ornithologists and birdwatchers have come to Selah for studies, bird counts, or just the pleasure of seeing so large a variety of species in an ideal setting. They often take advantage of the dormitories at The

BLACK-CAPPED VIREO *Vireo atricapilla*

Center to get an early start in the field and in the evening prepare their meals and talk by the fireplace. One of these birdwatchers happened to be my sister-in-law Margaret, who had been a staff member of the Austin Nature and Science Center for many years, working with children and on tours, educational programs, and publications. Her friend Mary Kay Sexton had been eager to introduce her to David Bamberger and arranged what turned out to be a pleasant dinner at her home with David and Margaret, among others, as guests.

Margaret was unaccustomed to such unchecked enthusiasm and storytelling. She could hardly have imagined that one day she would direct programs at Selah; travel five continents through exotic landscapes, observing birds, tigers, and butterflies; and above all befriend a remarkable network of naturalists, nature writers, and scientists. She would win national awards for conservation and have university awards and a middle-school greenhouse dedicated to her. That night at Mary Kay's, she had unwittingly met her future husband.

The Chiroptorium

LIKE DAVID, I had heard only vaguely of bat emergences before seeing one. I had pictured them as a kind of harmless tornado, a column formed by the uniform rush of particulate matter, black-winged mammals, night creatures with an accumulated baggage of cultural myths, literary roles, and comic book manifestations. It is easy to marvel at bats not only for the looping trajectory of their flight, their otherworldly senses, and their vast assortment of mask-like faces but also for their being inextricably bound to summer nights, going far back into childhood. When they flicker in the space between silhouetted trees, they create for themselves an envelope of sound, 360 degrees in three dimensions, seeing what we can't even imagine.

My first bat emergence bore little resemblance to David's. He had to crawl and battle through thick junipers for forty minutes with Andy Sansom to reach the mouth of Bracken Cave. He was rewarded with one of the world's most spectacular phenomena, twenty to thirty million Mexican free-tailed bats pouring for nearly an hour into the evening sky. I merely had to hop into the truck with Margaret and David, an after-dinner drink still in hand, and ride up Blue Ridge Drive past Carter Tank. We reached the cave, its mouth replicating an opening in stone facing the road, nestled in an ideal situation, surrounded by a limestone ridge near the top of a rise, with plenty of tree cover on both sides. The artificial structure had been covered with earth and then seeded with grass so that for the most part it looked entirely natural but was still quite accessible to visitors and researchers. That mid-May evening, two bat researchers from Boston University had arrived to work on a census project. Nick Hristov, a lean, young post-doc originally from Bulgaria, was assisted by Louise Allen, a pretty, dark-brown-haired graduate student working on her dissertation. They were staying at Recycle Cabin and planning a June return for a longer monitoring study of caves in the area. When we arrived, the bat scientists were busy setting up cameras and portable computer monitors on the banks beside the cave opening. David and Margaret pulled out folding chairs and sat comfortably by the roadside, passing a routine evening in their own rather vast backyard, except that they could bask in the satisfaction of seeing a huge gamble pay off. The novelty of the building, the largest artificial home ever designed explicitly for bats, brought extensive media attention to Selah and provided an educational focus for nature tour groups. It also provided, to Margaret's delight, a bat laboratory that brought biologists from American universities and from as far away as England and Japan.

David conceived the project with far reaching implications. "I wanted to demonstrate that a man-made habitat, of a significant size, could mitigate some of the damage man has done to Mother Nature with our shopping centers, subdivisions, and highways. I also wanted to provide an educational experience for visitors, perhaps motivate others to create a habitat of this scope for some other species."

I had first seen the bat cave when it resembled a massive underground garage, except that the interior contours and tunnels all had an organic quality, with a rough texture unlike that of the familiar, squared-off, poured concrete with supporting pillars. It was already three years old, and some serious worry had set in as to whether the eccentrically spent $180,000 would make the project "Bamberger's Folly." David says in retrospect, "Between you and me, I always knew they'd come. The question now is how many. Half a million? A million? If necessary, I could open the observation area and get in another 100,000. It's like an extra gas tank."

But David was less brash at the beginning. I wasn't steeped enough in bat migration patterns to have an opinion, but I figured that after three years the Bambergers could use some tangible signs of hope. On my first visit, David passed his flashlight beam over the vacant central dome close to the entry, and then we penetrated deeper to an ancillary dome linked to a third, egg-shaped chamber. The observation room that Margaret, ever science-minded, had suggested provided windows on all three chambers. On my initial viewing of the domed spaces—6,500 square feet for roosting bats—I was reminded of how Hadrian had built the Pantheon as a kind of dome-shaped birdhouse for deities, who also remained delinquent, though I suspect that his edifice housed more bats than did "Bamberger's Folly," with its then-meager number of transients. When news got around that Bamberger was building an artificial bat cave, there were those locals who, already suspicious of his innovative programs, conflated their vision of Selah, imagining a nudist colony and supposing that David was eradicating mosquitoes for the comfort of altogether vulnerable guests.

But five years later, I took the equivalent of box seating at a ballgame alongside the lively, though noticeably pale, Louise. Her pallor, I surmised, was the result of vegetarianism or her unusual form of nightlife or a combination of both. Her infrared thermal cameras picked up the heat that lingered in the sun-warmed trees, on the bright horizon, or on Nick's face, the monitor showing ghost-white images as twilight set in. The bats would be hot dots, a flurry of white gnats or crazed embers, the computer counting and verifying individuals by "flow-tracking" them.

Louise was assisting Nick with his census work. Her own studies involved monitoring the effects of stress on the growth and survival of pups. After the mothers had set off on their evening foraging, Louise would go to work on the pups, examining and measuring them at a bridge and a cave to make comparisons. She also monitored the health of adults at six sites—three bridges and three caves—taking blood and saliva samples. Texas is a particularly well-bat-endowed state, boasting thirty-two species that come in a variety of colors and sizes and with an array of peculiar ear and facial features, all substantiating such names as leaf-chinned, ghost-faced, and Rafinesque's big-eared. According to Merlin Tuttle's *Texas Bats*, the Mexican free-tailed bats, the champion colonizers, have developed a particular fondness for the Hill County area, with one and a half million laying claim to the Congress Avenue Bridge in Austin and two million enjoying an old Fredericksburg & Northern Railroad tunnel. Frio Cave has up to ten million residents, and the Eckert James River Bat Cave boasts six million.

When David and I were driving up to Oklahoma to see his brother Tom, we passed through a seemingly forsaken town west of Dallas, called Mineral Wells. It had experienced a series of reincarnations since the time of the Comanches and then of such ironically surnamed cattle barons as Charles Goodnight, Oliver Loving, and C. C. Slaughter. But the idea that mineral waters could cure arthritis transformed the town into a bizarre spa with a monolithic luxury hotel called The Baker, which had the extraordinary misfortune of opening two weeks after the 1929 crash. It featured suites with up to five rooms and seven baths. "That hotel is full of bats," David told me. "There is a lady who has made quite a reputation up here studying them." The lady's name is Amanda Lollar, and she founded a bat rehabilitation and education center called Bat World. I wondered if the luxury hotel wasn't just one preposterously large human-made bat habitat, like the Congress Avenue Bridge or the Fredericksburg & Northern Railroad tunnel. Of course, abandoned mines, barns, and even casinos have become bat homes. David described his cave to author Susan Sander as "the world's largest manmade habitat for the free-will use of wild mammals." That the cave had been intentionally located and built for bats for their "free-will use" was the critical difference.

Curiously, bats have been put to work for more than century now, and probably much longer, given that guano provides excellent fertilizer, not to mention a potential ingredient for powerful explosives. David told me that during World War I the military posted guards at bat caves, wary of the large German population in the area and of the potential for sabotage. In addition, in the early 1900s a clever doctor named Campbell, hoping to attract bats to help eradicate malaria, built towers on Mitchell Lake outside of San Antonio. Farmers knew that Mexican free-tailed bats have been particularly important for keeping in check the corn earworm and two types of budworm, thus protecting corn, cotton, and tomato crops. On a quite different front, during WWII there was a serious proposal, Project X-Ray, to use bats as a weapon of mass destruction. Thousands of bats, each carrying incendiary devices, were slated for release over Tokyo. The atomic bomb, however, trumped the bat firestorm. Jack Couffer's eerie book, *Bat Bomb: World War II's Other Secret Weapon*, is based on the project. After seven years, bats are happily employed at Selah in the "people ranching" business.

The idea of building a bat cave evolved through David's close association with Bat Conservation International (BCI). The initial Bracken Cave experience with Andy Sansom was transformative for David, who saw immediately the cave's potential for developing, through education and safe exposure, public enthusiasm for bats and eventually for nature conservation writ large.

In the early 90s, when David became single and found himself without Church's Fried Chicken, he asked Andy Sansom for advice about two organizations, the Texas Nature Conservancy and Bat Conservation International (BCI), that had approached him to serve on their boards. Andy thought David could make a serious contribution by joining the board of BCI and at the same time enjoy an enthusiastic group of people and their activities. Having developed a reputation, enhanced by Emily Hahn's article in *The New Yorker*, for land stewardship and environmental protection and for having already contributed $10,000 for the development of Eckert James River Bat Cave, David was enthusiastically welcomed to the BCI board.

At the time, BCI was trying to purchase Bracken Cave and surrounding land to allow access, but progress stagnated. With his background in real estate and business negotiations, David couldn't have come along at a better time. He put on his ranch get-up—his torn tee-shirt, jeans, and ball cap—and went out in his dusty pickup to the families' homes, door-to-door style, making them his genuine friends and at the same time preaching to them the idea of conservation. The acquisition was complicated, as David explained: "There were two different parties involved: the Reeh family, who didn't own Bracken Cave but owned 100% of the land around it, and then a fellow by the name of Irving Marbach, who, along with his two cousins, owned the cave itself, approximately five acres. Irving and those cousins also owned Frio, another bat-filled cave a hundred miles away. Now, I was able to buy the interest of Irving's cousins in both caves for BCI, but Irving was mining guano and kept his interest. BCI officials and lawyers began demanding that Irving wear respirators and get insurance, which only alienated him. It turned into a kind of squabble. What I accomplished was this: I went to Irving and said, 'I'll tell you what I'm going to do. You can have total ownership in Frio Cave in exchange for your one-third interest in Bracken.' So when he agreed, he owned all of Frio, and we owned Bracken. However, you can't protect the cave if you just own five acres. The object was to buy land from the Reeh family, who owned 2,000 acres, to create a perimeter around the cave. My task was then to make friends with the Reeh family. They didn't trust BCI or the lawyers coming down trying to throw their weight around. The land was held in undivided interest among a number of family members, including two minors, the children from a deceased sibling's second marriage. Now, if you own an undivided interest, no matter how small, you have control. The court had to speak for the children, but I ended up buying the interest of those two minors. That gave us leverage because with undivided interest we had just as much a say-so as any member of the Reeh family. Reeh family members were in their fifties and sixties with individual plans. I finally convinced them to divide the property and sell portions to BCI. It took me about five years to work it all out, negotiating the purchase of the land at Bracken for a bargain price. But you know what? I'm still friendly with that family. I was a pallbearer for Mrs. Reeh just a year ago."

Made chairman of Bracken Cave, David brought Leroy, Randy and others to clear juniper and make trails. He approached an organization of cavers called Bexar Grotto based in San Antonio. "Bexar Grotto was a group I recruited as volunteer stewards at Bracken Cave. They mowed the grass, cleared trails, and trimmed trees. Their volunteer work was worth $25,000 a year, easily."

David bonded with the group and began to wonder if he might not have a cave on his land, adding another important natural asset to Selah. "I'd bring the whole association, their wives and families, to the ranch all at my cost. Big chicken barbecue. Big tour. These guys came up, looked all over the ranch for what might be a cave but found nothing. We had a day when the weather changed. And it was suddenly much warmer down in the earth than the air temperature outside. My son-in-law Ernie was with me, and we saw a plume of steam going thirty feet in the air, right out of a crack in the ground. I told the Grotto guys about it, and they said that there had to be a cave. I took Leroy up there with the backhoe and bulldozer. I kept thinking of when Charlie was drilling for water, and the bit dropped forty feet. But when we didn't find anything, that's when I thought about a man-made one."

Why shouldn't David expect a cave at Selah? According to Eric Swanson's *Geo-Texas: A Guide to the Earth Sciences,* Texas has 3,000 documented ones, more than any other state. Besides, caves are ubiquitous in the Hill Country, with its layers of lifted limestone along a major fault, vulnerable over thousands of years to groundwater, which picks up carbon dioxide from the atmosphere as rain and seeps through decaying plants in the soil. The combination of water and CO_2 forms carbonic acid, which over thousands of years eats away rock to form fissures and eventually a subterranean network of gaps, cavities, and channels that grow into galleries. The slightly acidic water generally seeps and even flows, mainly from streams, into a vast body of porous rock, forming the Hill Country's all-important Edwards Aquifer, along the Balcones Fault zone. The recharging of the aquifer after a big rain is often dramatic. Swanson says,

> The cavernous Edwards limestone allows for swift underground movement of water. Water levels in San Antonio wells may jump ten feet or more in a single day following a heavy rain on the

recharge zone. Water doesn't actually flow to San Antonio in one day, but water in wells rises as a result of increased hydraulic pressure applied at the recharge zone, much as pouring water in one end of a U-shaped tube causes water at the other end to rise.

One night I walked across little Johnson City, past LBJ's modest boyhood home, to the LBJ Center to listen to a lecture on cave biodiversity and creatures known as troglobitic fauna that exist somewhere under our feet in yet-to-be-discovered caves. I sat in an audience of eight people and listened to a cave expert characterize "undescribed" species, as they are called, creatures never seen before: spider, millipede, and silverfish, their whitish translucence something like an underground negative of their above-ground relatives. More appealing were the blind salamanders, ghostly catfish, cave ceiling crickets, beetles, and crevice frogs, accompanied by an unfortunate rattlesnake misdirected into permanent darkness. These worlds of endangered and, until recently, unknown species can exist even in urban areas, and environmentalists sometimes hold up the plans of developers callous to the plight of translucent critters.

A natural cave might be discovered one day at Selah, but David, always an initiator, began picking the brains of experts he'd met through BCI to get opinions on the feasibility of attracting bats to a human-made bat cave. When the experts couldn't argue against such a cave, he began to conceive an inexpensive poured-concrete structure, rectilinear like an underground garage. As chance would have it, though, he met Jim Smith, an ingenious—if eccentric—industrial engineering school dropout with a name that seemed like a hasty and inadequate alias. His medium build, prep-school good looks, and dirty-blond hair somehow conspired to disguise his considerable physical energy and stamina. Margaret had met Jim through the Zahners, mutual friends in Highlands, North Carolina. At that time, he had been living for thirteen years as the reclusive caretaker of a friend's log cabin in the Blue Ridge Mountains. It had become his refuge, where he could flee his northeastern gentry origins, Jesuit schooling, and stints at Cornell and the Rhode Island School of Design.

While David and Margaret visited the Zahner home in Tucson, Jim happened to be passing through, having taken up nomadic life in his custom-built camper, "the land yacht." He cut the roof off a Dodge van and replaced it with a top that he described as "a cross between a 747 and a cabin cruiser." David, passionate since childhood about design and motor vehicles, was blown away. "That van of his, you should have seen it. It was a work of art in itself. He designed all sorts of stuff, Herculean, superman stuff." Besides unusual construction work, Jim had done lighting design and photography, calling himself diffidently a *Lebenskünstler*, literally, "life-artist" in German, one who lives his life aesthetically.

The quality of Jim's imaginative work and his apparent rootlessness set David scheming, and within a day he said to him, apropos the land yacht, "If you can build something like this, I'll bet you could build a bat cave." The chance to design and build the largest-ever artificial bat habitat caused a change of Jim's plans, one so abrupt it would have caught even the Delphic Oracle off guard. He pondered the proposition for a month, wise enough to know that innovation and complexity beget entanglements and that once he started, he'd be in for the long haul. Still, such offers didn't come along every day. Besides, Kurt Vonnegut's aphorism was etched into his soul: "Unusual travel suggestions are like dancing lessons from God." He altered his Homeric land yacht course and reached Selah in the beautiful month of March, in the perfect season to start such a project, spring and the long Texas summer stretching before him.

Jim's first task was to learn bat basics from obliging BCI and university experts, who dressed him up in boots, a protective suit, and gloves with rubber bands at the sleeves and furnished him with a respirator before leading him into chambers filled with ammonia and waxy guano and lined with dark knots of Mexican free-tails. Jim saw immediately that the bats hung tightly packed on inner-dome ceilings and emerged from a broad cave mouth. He was counseled to add texture to the interior, allowing the bats footholds, and to provide appropriate dimensions, of both height and width, to accommodate a massive population.

Wanting an expeditious project, David led Jim to his preferred site, which met one of David's requirements and one of the scientists': that it be on the ranch's tour route and within a quarter mile of a body of water. Building a cave from the ground up, Jim realized, would be easiest if it were erected in a small canyon so that the soil could be filled in along the edges of the slopes and then cover over the structure. The spot above Carter Tank fit everyone's specifications.

It took Jim only two weeks to draw up his organic design for three contiguous domes, including calculations on how to build them of ferrous cement. Coincidentally, three months earlier he had been on Orcas Island in San Juan, building a domed sauna to be covered with earth. He had been working specifically on its natural lighting, using hollowed logs. The structural framing of the sauna was concrete reinforcing bar (rebar) and chicken wire. A community party was arranged, with neighbors slathering on cement with hands and trowels: Tom Sawyer without the trickery. Jim would now make use of some parallels, but the scale of the bat cave, its domes twenty feet high and forty feet in diameter, would dwarf the San Juan project.

As soon as David approved the plan, Leroy, no nonsense, arrived with his bulldozer and carved out the canyon, even though he most likely doubted the wisdom of the endeavor. He leveled the canyon's bottom to pour a three-thousand-foot foundation. At any given time, two to five Mexicans were contributing their hard work and high spirits to the bat-friendly enterprise, and one can only imagine their trying to explain the cave to families back home. The structure took nine months to complete: "the classic gestation period," as Jim would call it, and David took full advantage of that time for people ranching, featuring the construction site for BCI meetings and media invitations that were eagerly accepted.

Months before I'd ever spoken to Jim Smith, photographs of the rebar skeleton with its mesh skin underneath intrigued me. The three domes, in differing shapes and with connecting tunnels, were photographed at twilight while illuminated from the interior. The rhythms in the bar spacing and the feminine curvature of the domes were sculptural. Jim had taken the photographs. "I like to build things that are nice to photograph, so that I was very careful in the construction and the positioning of the rebar to create something that was a beautiful structure. . . . I took shots at various stages, even when it was just the rebar and looked like an aviary. Flocks of birds at the end of the day would perch on all those bars. And when I put the stucco on, then it became a habitat for butterflies."

Since there were no precedents for such a structure, the process itself was at times organic, artistic in itself, discovery through making. "I had a design that probably any formal architecture builder would have laughed at. It was basically a footprint in a profile. The rest of it just evolved organically. You can't know how the intersections are going to work until you do it. So you work for the concept and the spaces you need. Then you let the form evolve." The form was solidified using a process called "Gunite," a four-hundred-p.s.i. compressor shooting five hundred cubic yards of concrete over seven and a half miles of rebar.

For the self-proclaimed *Lebenskünstler*, the satisfaction was in the beauty of the project, something rarely appreciated in a utilitarian society. Such beauty is an extravagance, for which Smith paid with fourteen-hour days. He was fortunate to be in the position to choose his projects. Jim Smith has never returned to see an emergence. He joked, "It's on my life-list."

Building an artificial bat cave was just the sort of oddball story the press adored. "That bat cave," David explained, "hit at a lethargic time in the news. Everything wasn't peaches and roses, and the media is always looking for interesting stuff. I wanted the microphone, to be able to talk, to give my viewpoints. That bat cave, once again, took us to another level."

David needed a catchy word for the one-of-a-kind habitat. Margaret and David's son created one by fusing *Chiroptera*, the bat's scientific order, with *auditorium*. David said, "When I heard Chiroptorium, I thought, damn, it's not only right; it's brilliant." The media, including *People*, CNN, the "Voice of America" radio program, and newspapers across America and in England, picked up immediately on the project, often and predictably dubbing it "batty."

Even close friends like David's former business associate Kovel, who "knew nothing from bats," thought that bats had to find their own home. The more screwball-sounding the project became—"Bamberger's Folly" and smirking references to *Field of Dreams:* "If you build it, they will come"—the more giddy David became, joking about family disputes: Margaret wanting to turn the cave into a dinosaur display and David saying that it would serve as his enormous wine cellar.

Ironically, David's Chiroptorium garnered more media attention than Bracken Cave itself, the extraordinary natural wonder that inspired it. While building the Chiroptorium and awaiting the arrival of his own bats, David worked tirelessly for BCI and Bracken Cave. In the late 1990s, Margaret had joined him in developing visits and talks at the cave. Despite all that David had done for Bracken, friction began to develop between him and his fellow BCI board members. He explained, "Margaret and I organized a thing called 'Members-Only Night.' We had four nights during the summer when groups of up to fifty BCI members and invited scientists and environmentalists could come to see this magnificent site. We even brought people from Europe. But it took me two years of wrangling and haggling with the management of BCI to make the program work."

BCI lawyers worried about liability while others were concerned that groups of fifty would have a negative impact on the land and the bat colony. Above all, BCI didn't want to use their resources for handling reservations. David and Margaret overcame these objections by managing the program entirely themselves, using Selah's telephones and fax machines. Over time, David would insist that "Members-Only Night" was the most successful marketing plan for a conservation agency anywhere.

With the enormous popularity of the "Members-Only Night" and aided by a sizable grant, BCI's ambitions shifted 180 degrees to what David called disdainfully "Disneyland at Bracken Cave" in an interview with Christopher Anderson of the *San Antonio Express-News.* A prestigious architectural firm had been commissioned to draw up elaborate plans for a "state-of-the-art interpretive center" for educating the public

about the habits and benefits of bats. Plans called for expanded parking, sanitary facilities, a café, a bookstore, and a gift shop. From the
beginning, David opposed such development and argued in a counter
proposal,

> As I watched that rare and spectacular show of nature, which
> has thrilled every one of us, I wondered just why we would want
> to risk it for a grandiose development plan. The experience is
> completely natural now. Natural as few places are, and certainly
> few places readily accessible to millions of people. This makes
> Bracken Cave so rare as to be absolutely unique. Whatever we do
> here cannot improve the habitat.

David follows this argument up with a far more moderate eight-point plan
advocating the purchase of the entire Reeh ranch and only constructing
modest visitor's facilities at the highway entrance, a mile from the cave.
By contrast, BCI intended to raise 18.5 million dollars to realize designs
that in one version included an elevator into the cave.

David, in the end, was the lone dissenting voice on the board, and
when the vote came up for adopting the ambitious plans, BCI members
convinced him that the project would proceed with or without him but
that they hoped for a board consensus to help with fundraising. In what
David described as a "weak moment," he voted "yea," a vote he would
deeply regret and in effect later retract. He began to assail the proposal
publicly and lobbied "Members-Only Night" attendees to write letters to
protect the untouched beauty of Bracken. David expressed his objections
to the Bracken Cave plan in *Texas Monthly* and later in the *San Antonio
Express-News*. However, in a letter to Sarah McCabe, an editor at *Texas
Monthly*, David expressed his objections most bluntly:

> I'm not opposed to public access to Bracken Cave. I am opposed
> to making a business out of it. Opposed to 1,000 visitors per night,
> opposed to spending $15+ million in building and improvements,

opposed to the environmental disturbance of the land, opposed to exploiting Mother Nature in every place we discover her hidden treasures, opposed to $7–10 admission fees, opposed to losing the focus of BCI, drifting away from a successful mission and getting into a business that's competitive and expensive—one in which no one at BCI has experience.

BCI halted David's activities at Bracken. In response, David felt compelled to make a statement by resigning. "I feel I must leave Bat Conservation International or sacrifice my principles." David told me on numerous occasions how proud he is of his accomplishments at Bracken Cave, and clearly the plaques from BCI attest to his valuable contributions. With his entirely independent project, the Chiroptorium, he remained committed to bat conservation, and I was about to experience an emergence he created.

Sitting in the small, darkening canyon with Louise and her illuminated screen, I was curious about why the bats emerge all at once, what triggers them. She told me that it was probably anti-predator behavior, as in schools of baitfish or penguin parades. The bats come out in huge columns or a swirl, but then they disperse, flying remarkable distances to forage. Interestingly, they all also return at about the same time, dropping their wings and flashing into their cave. One bat sped out of the cave and missed the camera. Then two or three sparked white through the white thermal images of grass. The next bat tore left. Louise said, in playful intimacy with them, "They are being naughty. They're turning tonight. They are naughty bats."

Suddenly the bats began racing out as if a wind tunnel propelled them. The emergence wasn't at all what I expected. These Mexican free-tailed bats travel so fast, so high, and then so far. It was exhilarating. I turned to see David and Margaret watching their creation: what had been seven thousand bats in a five-minute emergence at peak season the year before was now twenty-seven thousand over twenty minutes. The number would only grow as the year progressed. I took vicarious delight in success so long-awaited, some fifteen years after David's divorce and his joining BCI to recover.

Later, discussing the Chiroptorium, David ventured that he could construct another at the bargain-basement price of $50,000, and certainly no project should be initiated without consideration of possible ancillary income production, in this case from people-ranching and fertilizer, not to mention a potential bomb shelter. "I got a guy in West Texas who is going to build one and a guy in Marble Falls who *wants* to build one, based on the same concept as ours."

TEXAS SNOWBELL *Styrax platanifolius* var. *texanus*

The Texas Snowbell Story

IF YOU ARE lucky enough to find a Texas snowbell, it usually looks like a modest shrub masked by a variety of saplings and bushes. If given the chance, it grows into a very attractive flowering tree. It still clings to existence on sculpted cliff walls in gorges along the Nueces and Devil's rivers near the Mexican border. David became obsessed with removing the plant from the critically endangered species list. While, on the face of it, this project may not seem particularly heroic, the implications are far reaching in the second largest American state with the smallest percentage of public lands. "Private land rights in Texas are the sacred cow," an environmentalist told me, and in the region where the snowbell grows ranchers are particularly suspicious of the Endangered Species Act and federal intervention on their lands. David went straight to the private landowners, searching out new Texas snowbell colonies, growing the plant himself, and reintroducing it where the federal government isn't welcomed. David invited me on a snowbell search in the region where the Edwards Plateau gives way to Chihuahuan desert to the south and the Trans-Pecos Mountains to the west.

David, Steven, and I headed west in an emergency-response-red, four-wheel drive Ford pickup. The new ranch acquisition, though second-hand, made David cringe, costing more than Leroy's bulldozer. David had just recently learned to tolerate air conditioning, something he considered a waste, particularly with gas prices soaring into a dimension once unthinkable to Americans. When he turned seventy-five, he started allowing others, if not himself, this occasional comfort in the Texas heat. We pulled in to a grocery store in Fredericksburg, not far from Hill Country Memorial Hospital where Margaret spent a good part of

October until stabilized enough to receive home hospice care. Pandora had given birth to two puppies in France, and on asking Margaret to name one the assignment required almost no thought; she said Snowbell. It was the first time I'd even heard of the endangered plant species, and now my dog had become its namesake.

Setting out with David on the Texas snowbell recovery project put me in mind of first Hes', then his passion for trees. On the south side of the ranch house gallery, David built sets of two-tiered shelving with snowbell plants ranging from seedling sprouts to two-year-old saplings. This modest arrangement represented the only successful nursery for the endangered snowbell recovery operation for the entire state of Texas. It stood just steps from his bedroom, and he doted on the seedlings, kept in filtered sunlight thanks to several neighboring oaks. It was brisk physical work for anyone, much less a seventy-seven-year-old, to survey the banks of the Devil's and Nueces rivers in spring, collect seeds in September, grow saplings, and then plant new colonies in November, all the while keeping careful records of survivorship in each corral. The timing of the spring trip was a considerable gamble since the period when the snowbell blossomed varied by weeks from year to year, depending on moisture levels and the length of the winter. The probability of seeing new colonies on the cliffs without the advantage of blooms approached zero.

The Texas snowbell is beautiful in the spring, with its delicate clusters of downward-hanging bell-shaped blossoms, egg-yolk-yellow pistils and stamens only partially visible. The blossoms eventually produce their drupe seeds, so precious to David's project. The small tree grows only ten to fifteen feet tall and has heart-shaped, light green leaves with pale pubescence that in a breeze gives a revealing shimmer. But for the most part, without the shimmer and the blossoms, the Texas snowbell is almost impossible to distinguish from other vegetation and then even more difficult to find since their colonies are very rare and often small. There is a far more common variety, the sycamore-leaf snowbell (*Styrax platanifolius*), which is native to eastern parts of the Hill Country. The varieties resemble each other, except that the underleaf of the sycamore-leaf snowbell does not have the frosted look.

Our group began assembling at a Rocksprings diner where the walls were densely populated with taxidermy animals and the shelves cluttered with African woodcarvings. Laura Sanchez, a botanist for the Department of Defense, arrived from Fort Hood, and Susan Sander, from the Texas Forest Service, showed up with a visiting forestry expert from the Czech Republic named Vladimir Wlada. Colleen and her husband Scott Gardner would meet us at the Smith Ranch. We would be joined later by others from the Texas Parks and Wildlife Department and the press, planning a photo shoot of model-like, former Peace Corps volunteer, Colleen.

Del Rio and the Amistad Reservoir, near the Mexican border, appeared stark to me while caught in dense NAFTA traffic, glare, and dust from the red, flat land. The strict surveillance of the border patrol didn't help my initial sense of desolation, but this was also the country of the legendary Judge Roy Bean and the courtroom where he presided, his own Jersey Lily Saloon, colorful American lore in itself. Soon the land revealed more relief and the brush vegetation appeared more varied, along with the famous Texas range grasses and then stands of live oaks, bald cypresses, and pecans nearer water. We'd eventually come to the clear, green river cutting cliffs, turns, and small canyons into the limestone. Mosses, ferns, shrubs and vines lined springs and seeps.

We came to Dobbs Run, owned by Earnest and Paula Smith, and enjoyed reasonably comfortable sleeping quarters and kitchen facilities built primarily for hunting groups and some vacationers. Protective bars over some of the windows were bent apart. I was told that a steady traffic of illegal Mexicans passed through the property and they experienced some problems with theft, including a stolen water truck, which turned out to be a mistake since it leaked a trail directly to the thieves. We met Tommy Sergeant, an eighty-six year old former county judge with just a high-school education. Tommy was a rabid Democrat, going back to the days when the Republicans didn't have an organized party in Texas.

Tommy worked as secretary-treasurer of the Marfa Electrical Co-op before becoming a judge. When the forester from the Czech Republic was introduced, Tommy demanded, "Say that again. Did you say Republican?" The poor forester's fate was sealed. He'd been dubbed "The Republican."

That afternoon we drove out to Ken Boester's Bluff Creek Ranch, where a broad bend in the Nueces created a rock face with numerous ledges harboring shrubs. This was an area where Texas snowbells had been discovered before, and it was important for the group to know if they were, in fact, in bloom. Most of us stood on the bank looking with binoculars across the river at the cliff face while Steven and Scott walked across a dam and climbed to a spot where they knew snowbells were growing. There has been much debate over why the snowbell chooses to live in inaccessible areas along rivers. Some botanists contend they thrive on rising moisture along the river cliff face, but the Selah crew believes that, yes, the moisture is important but they survive because they grow where sheep, goats, and wildlife can't reach them. The report hollered across the river wasn't at all good; the blossoms were well behind schedule. Even with Global Positioning and careful scanning, it was difficult to spot the known plants.

By evening I felt like I'd joined a National Geographic team: strategy discussed over maps, teams assigned to territories for the most efficient coverage—but then, predictably, the seriousness deteriorated. The Republican put away a least a six pack, and the rest of us did our share, David launching into a story of how on some of David's San Antonio property a school group stumbled across one of Santa Ana's cannons used against the Alamo and the teacher claimed it, winning a court battle against David.

The next day started with Scott Gardner cooking bacon and frying eggs in the residual grease, declaring loudly that our breakfast was certified by the American Heart Association. We all sensed, however, that finding new colonies appeared hopeless. We split up into groups, ours consisting of Laura Sanchez, Steven, David, and me. Laura, a botanist in her thirties, knew Steven from hiring him for summer internships at Fort Hood.

Supporting two armored divisions, Fort Hood is the largest active military base in the country, covering a total of 339 square miles. Laura said that such a huge tract of land would require monitoring by federal law for the protection of endangered species. This is a live ammunition training area for artillery and heavy armored vehicles designed to trample landscapes and change the topography into craters. Even in this war-training zone, the cowbird had to be controlled. Laura and Steven worked together on oak wilt and no doubt surveyed plants and birds.

We found our unexplored portion of the river and emptied out of the Ford so that Steven could test drive across the river, plowing an impressive wave in front of him. He returned to get us. The river widened from the cliff face on the far side, and Steven waded out into the water up to his shoulders, almost six feet of his huge body, peering with binoculars. Finally growing impatient, he crossed to inspect the pathless base of the cliff and its top. We found nothing.

We explored another tract, with small tributaries, opportunistic feathery bald cypresses seeming to cool their roots in running water and small gravel islands. Leroy would say that the beautiful trees were just pipes sucking out the water. I found them majestic, with their pyramidal shape, the broad trunk base tapering upward, their roots "kneeing" out of pools. The next day, we planned to spend the morning covering new creek beds looking for snowbells, knowing that our chances of spotting any were slim, and then, so that the trip would not be wasted, begin inspection of the reintroduction sites. We started at our original stop on the Nueces and split up into small groups. David and I crossed the river over the dam and ascended the side of the cliff of the Nueces.

While we ducked branches and pressed through underbrush, I asked David questions, particularly regarding how he got into a snowbell recovery project. I knew he had worked on the Murray plum in the region and was intrigued by an aquatic plant called Little Aguja Creek pondweed, an endangered species that manages to miraculously survive in one location under harsh conditions in West Texas, but I wondered what drew him to raising and reintroducing the Texas snowbell. "I'll show you a plaque I have hanging in the living room when we get back," he said. "It was an award in 1994 from the Nature Conservancy at a large annual affair in San Antonio, and it had this color photograph of a Texas Snowbell." I remembered seeing it with a clutter of plaques. David recalled, "Shortly before I received the award this a guy gave me one snowbell seed. One seed? How ridiculous. But that picture and that award said to me, 'Goddamn it, Bamberger, that's another thing you can do.' That's really when it became important. Margaret came into my life, and with someone like her who knew the science and the biology, she could go with me and participate. She and I camped out here a few times. We met people and started working."

David's Texas snowbell recovery program had been in the works for nearly ten years, predating the Chiroptorium. It took nearly twenty-five years for a viable effort to emerge for the reintroduction of the scimitar-horned oryx in the sub-Saharan desert. What became abundantly clear during my time at Selah was that conservation is as much about perseverance as it is foresight. Unfortunately, with changes in government, the ability to sustain programs for a healthy environment is routinely undermined by pleasing the voters with ever-popular tax cuts. Programs come and go, creating waste rather than sustained effort to understand and remedy problems. Environmental legislation, such the Endangered Species Act, is forever in danger, as it is subject to repeal with a shift in the political winds.

Part of what sustains David's projects and attention is younger people and conservationists, and Steven would inherit the Snowbell reintroduction program for his masters' thesis and perhaps even for a Ph.D. project at the University of Texas. Besides the Texas Parks and Wildlife studies of a natural snowbell colony in the Nature Conservancy's Dolan Falls Preserve, there is little government effort for sustaining or augmenting the Texas snowbell population. It's hard not to sympathize with under-staffed Parks and Wildlife personnel, whose resources are stretched thin and regarded by some extremist private landowners as agents of a socialist force aiming to nationalize their lands. Even the more moderate ranch owners don't want their lands policed. In an interview for *Texas Studies Annual*, David explained,

> The Trans-Pecos Heritage Association was formed by private landowners because the U.S. Fish and Wildlife Service made a big announcement that they were going to create a million-acre park around Ft. Davis, and then the Nature Conservancy announced that they had found the (endangered) Little Aguja Creek pond-weed out here. . . . So, if a rancher has some weed he's never noticed before, hell, he's afraid to let anyone on his property.

David went on to say that the landowners were "almost storing up food and guns and all." As David contended with the Endangered Species Act, many private landowners do not recognize the economic potential of attracting nature tourism through the rare species on their land.

Radical conservatives have said to David that they wouldn't mind if he wound up with a bullet in his head, but being a private landowner himself, with success in the business world and notoriety as a conservationist, many private landowners in West Texas would listen to David's propositions regarding surveys for snowbell colonies and reintroduction of plants. "The first four years I was making contacts. That was all legwork. It was like going back to my Kirby days. It was kind of door-to-door. I'd go to a ranch that was in that part of the world and introduce myself and show them magazine stories. Tell them, 'I'm a private landowner, just like you. I think we should be proactive and do something that we can hang our hat on.' I just kind of networked through it. Then I looked through herbariums and talked to scientists who might have spotted one of these plants or knew where some were."

David soon discovered small colonies of plants on private West Texas land and recovered seeds at the end of summer. There were very few at first, and he decided to hire professionals to help him. "I tried two high profile nurseries and a botanist." He explained, "They didn't produce one plant, not one, and those seeds were rare at the time. We took the seeds to them. They didn't grow one damned plant. The botanists haven't put their feet out on the dirt. I had so many disappointments on that. I started doing them myself. Now the San Antonio Botanical Center was appointed by the Department of Interior to be in charge of the recovery project for the Texas snowbell. They propagated a few and put in a few dozen or so, almost all of which are dead now. And the biggest reason they are dead is that they didn't put a strong protective mesh around them and now most of them are gone. We put a corral around them that will be there for fifty years or more. Nothing can get in to eat them, except a mouse. The second reason they didn't survive is because at the time those scientists believed that the plant wanted to be on the side of a cliff or in the most God-awful place. I believed just the opposite. It happened to survive in a place where the deer and goats didn't get it. I've got more people on my side of the coin now. I have planted hundreds and have thirteen new landowners involved on the watershed of the Nueces and Devil's rivers. I'm getting up to 75,000 or more acres to work on now."

There we were on private land, David leading me along the pathless rim of the cliff. Twice our conversation was interrupted as furious bees targeted me specifically for some inadvertent trespass, stinging my hands and neck, while David, utterly unscathed, watched my panicked dance. While I recovered in a pasture on top of the cliff, David pointed out how ranchers had uprooted old cedars with a tractor and chain, decades ago he speculated, given the extent of rot on the trunks. We then continued on to pay homage to the one snowbell shrub we'd spotted the first evening, if only to offer me the satisfaction of seeing that in fact they do exist in the wild. However, when David wasn't leading me into bee attacks, he was getting us stranded on the cliff face. I have no idea what we would have done if Steven hadn't fortuitously shown up out of the blue. Steven calmly crossed the dam and then directed us to foot and hand holds, and then allowed us to stand on his shoulders to ease us off the rock. Laura was fully prepared to watch two fools tumble into the river.

Still feeling unjustly stung and then seeing David entirely unflustered by our rock climb, I couldn't suppress the creeping suspicion his bravado might be fine for him but clearly dangerous for me, whereas he'd see my inexperience as a distraction to his snowbell search. Steven said we needed to move quickly as Scott and Colleen had cornered an enormous diamond-backed rattler under a rock upriver. I thought, okay, my trip to West Texas could hardly be complete without a rattlesnake. While I'd had no warning about bees and following David on the cliff face, I'd been thoroughly advised to the dangers of breaking my leg in loose rocks and annoying rattlesnakes. Steven was taking us to see the godfather of rattlers.

We crossed the whitish river stones of a tributary to the Nueces, another gorgeous spot with water dripping down in the shadows of exotic-looking vertical cliff walls with languorous vegetation hanging down from the rim of the mesa, cool mosses and lichen. We saw Scott, Colleen, Susan Sander, Laura, and The Republican all gathered around the shady bank. David was as stricken with joy as a prospector at a find or a kid confronted with some dreamed-of, but unlikely gift. The "rattler" turned out to be the largest colony of Texas snowbells found on private property, and the second largest known, second only to the one at the Dolan Falls Preserve. The whole group, with an ineffable glow of satisfaction, had assembled in what seemed like a natural garden of Texas snowbells.

The colony had been Scott Gardner's find, which he recalled to us with his typical understatement, rubbing his dark goatee. "Susan and I were walking pretty much right below the bluff where it starts to angle out there towards the creek." He pointed downriver. "We were walking right at the base of this vertical wall. And we knew we were in a pretty good location. We saw water dripping off that vertical wall and we got to a little place where there was a really nice pool of water in the creek. It looked really inviting to Susan, and she just needed to take a dip. She asked that I continue on a little bit and it wasn't much more than fifteen yards beyond that that I just looked down and I was almost standing on four or five snowbells, little bitty guys. At first, I was in disbelief. I thought surely they were going to be saplings of some other tree, but when I looked ahead I saw the one that had the flowers on it. It was the larger one in blossom that gave them away. There were so many of them on the ground. I looked up here along the bluff and pretty much right above me was this big one. It was right then that I started shouting to Susan, to everyone."

Colleen heard the shouting through the trees, and Susan abruptly ended her soothing dip, still buttoning up, dripping, and disheveled when confirming the find. Scott had immediately recognized a significant feature of the site besides its size: regeneration was in progress. "It's so rare that you see regeneration. So often you see the mothers along that vertical wall, but when they start to have their saplings, deer or goats quickly eat them up." Scott walked into a colony of eighty-seven plants, triggering excited talk about how to reveal the information, what studies could be conducted, and even setting up witness cameras and exposing some of the plants to see what sorts of wildlife might want to eat them. They were not at all on a cliff face, but on the vulnerable bank of the river, confirming to some degree David's view that Texas snowbells would choose less inaccessible terrain if they could avoid foragers there. Ken Boester told David that he removed the sheep long ago and anthrax killed 80% of the deer population, providing a reasonable explanation for the survival of the colony.

Spirits couldn't have been higher for the rest of the field trip. That evening we all congregated on a perch-type porch built on the roof of the main compound, drinking wine and beer, talking excitedly—that is, when the irrepressible birdwatchers weren't pointing out birds: a hooded oriole, a summer tanager, and a vermilion flycatcher. Having such flashy birds in itself seemed like particularly good fortune.

The final day was reserved for Colleen's photo shoot in the morning, checking on snowbell corrals, and exploring new sights on the Devil's River. I went with David, Scott, Colleen, and the photojournalist to a reintroduction site. We piled into a dented beige Ford pickup, and I chose a mounted bench over the cab with a welded tray for ammunition and a rack for steadying a rifle. The truck was in essence a mobile hunting stand, a killing machine. I had lost my hat in all the excitement at discovering the snowbells and wrapped my head with a tee shirt, making us look, while turning up dust on the desert tract, a bit like the Taliban.

We climbed up into a shaded crevice, and just above us in an even more inaccessible spot was a Texas snowbell tree in full bloom. Usually, they grow ten to fifteen feet at most; this one had to be closer to twenty feet. One could see, without having to say it, the importance of saving it.

I asked David how many plants he had reintroduced and what his goals were. "I can give you the exact figure. I have 254 plants alive in the ground now. Soon our greenhouse will start to function, and we have about 2,000 seeds in the refrigerator. That will be enough to finish my project, which aims to plant 500. The third year out, 2009, we'll make sure that they are all alive. I did get a little help from Washington and Texas, but to be candid with you, I'm still a volunteer."

We all moved down along the riverbed to prosperous-looking snowbells in protective corrals. The journalist unpacked his equipment, positioned Colleen in nurturing poses, and used me as a studio lighting stand. I stood on a smooth rock outcropping and held the flash pack aimed at Colleen and the saplings. I tried to image a grove of trees twenty or thirty years ahead. There was plenty of sunlight, but the flash was to fill in, to glint away shadows. Colleen was beaming, blue-eyed, blonde, lending her natural beauty to the story of a tree. Who would imagine the Texas snowbells could be so glamorous?

Hes' Trees

....

DAVID BAMBERGER, speaking to ranch visitors near a grove he planted close to Hes' Country Store, April 29, 2005:

This old barn-like building to the left is called Hes' Country Store. Because her name was Hester, everyone called her Hes. She lived very simply. Everything I inherited that relates to a love of the land, of nature, I got from her. She lived on four acres in the midst of the Amish people. I told you she ate nothing that was manufactured. She got her eggs from the chickens that scratched in her dirt yard. She got her meat, vegetables, and fruits from the land. When her youngest son left home with a twelve-month old baby and no money—that's me—she was saddened. The time with her children seemed all too short. I'm down here in Texas, and I've got this ranch that you've been visiting today. She was not world-traveled or anything; she didn't like to travel. She was just ninety-four pounds and 4'10."

She called me on the phone. Now, I'm fifty-one years old when this happens. She said, "David, I have to speak to you." I said, "Let me sit down, Mom." "You don't need to sit. I'm coming down there." I said, "Well, hey, we can talk on the phone for now." "No, we can't talk on the phone. Don't you know that I'm on a seven-party telephone line?" Six other people had the same number. That's how far back in the country she was. So I said, "Great. Come on down. With the kids and all, we'll have a wonderful time." So she arrived, and I took her straight to the ranch. She was pacing the floor; she never paced the floor. I said, "Mom, what's the matter with you?"

"Well, David, I told you I had to speak with you." I said, "Well, let's sit down on the patio." "No. No. No. I want to sit with the cows." This woman liked every animal. She loved the birds and the cows, the chickens and the hawks. So I brought her to where this bus is sitting right now.

This was a dirt road at the time, and we were feeding cattle over here on the other side. We sat on a feed trough. Buddy had fifty to a hundred cattle in this pasture. Where my mother lived in Ohio, the Amish people had a team of horses, sometimes three; they had twelve hogs; they had a milk cow, two or three beef animals; and the farms were 200 acres. So 5,500 acres was unheard of in private ownership up there, especially in my mother's world. These cows start coming up from every direction, from out of the brush, out of the valley, out of the trees. They were licking on her coat and licking on her leg. They were pushing in, and I grew a little nervous. I thought these cows would get the best of us, but they didn't. I said, "Mom, what is that you wanted to talk about." She said, "Oh yes. David, how big is this ranch?" I was pretty proud. I puffed my chest out. "5,500 acres, Ma." "5,500 acres?" she shouted. This was bad. See, my mother was very poor. No one should own this kind of stuff. She looked around; she'd never seen this many cows. Most she had seen at one time was five or six. "How many cows do you have?" I was still pretty proud. I stuck out my chest. "Oh, gosh, I don't know." "You don't know?"

Boy, am I in trouble. Well, there's one hundred and fifty or one hundred and seventy five altogether. "'Now let's see, David. You've got that lovely house in San Antonio. And I really like the ranch house up here." By that time her youngest son was getting pissed off. So I stood and I said, "Mom, just what the hell is this all about?" She says, "Son, you look at me. I want you to look at me and tell me. Did you get all this honest?" My own mother came one thousand five hundred miles to have some assurance that I hadn't robbed a bank or run drugs.

She said, "Well, I'll tell you, with all you have I'm never going to be a burden on you." I said, "Mom, don't talk that way. No way in the world you're ever going to be a burden on me." "And I'll tell you something else, Davy. You nor Tom, you're not putting me into none of those warehouse rest homes. No," she said, "When my time comes, I'm going to walk out of my house, and I'm going to visit my trees." She said, "If you ever try to reach me and you can't, you look in my trees." I said, "Mom, don't talk that way."

"Across that road there I'm going to build a log cabin." "Oh," she said. 'Why are you doing that?" I said, "I don't know. Maybe a little gathering place on the ranch. Maybe a museum." "I'd love to see that," she said. "Would you want any of my things?"

That was my last personal conversation with my mother. I put her on the plane the next day, and five months later the neighbors called me and said, "Dave, you need to come up here. We didn't notice any activity around your mother's house. We found her down with her trees. She had a wildflower bouquet in one hand and a pair of shears in the other."

When Mom woke up that morning, she knew she had just a very short time to live. This is how I know: She had no radio, no television, no newspaper. She lived in kind of a shack. She didn't have post-ems. She didn't have scotch tape. Or thumbtacks. She took envelopes that come in the mail from the church or from wherever. She cut those envelopes in strips. And she left sixty-seven messages. "These chairs were made by your uncle Alf in Hartford City, Indiana, 1892. They are very old. This cradle, your great grandmother slept in this as she came here from the old country. And this knife I bought for 15¢ when I was twelve years old. I still use it to pick dandelions. This lantern, your grandfather used it when he worked on the railroad. . . ." The other sixty-three, plus those four messages, had been tied with string to these items. When I walked into her little house, eleven of these messages had already drifted to the floor.

People Ranching

DAVID TOLD HIS fable-like story of Hes' death hundreds of times to groups of children who had come to Selah to be exposed, often for the first time, to open Hill Country landscape: to study nature, learn about balances in the ecosystems, and grasp some principles of conservation. The portrayal of Hes' poverty was an invention taken from David's early years. "I've said it this way so many times that for me it's true." Keenly aware that science and nature's plight alone will not necessarily capture the imaginations of the kids, he tailors his personal story, the human side, to inspire students to learn about their own heritage, to take pride in grandparents and ancestors, no matter how modest, and Hes herself as the example could hardly be presented as more deprived of the material wealth that is worshipped in American society. The students also deduce that you can have humble beginnings and ultimately own 5,500 acres that in turn is dedicated to unarguably the most important cause possible, given that nothing survives without healthy earth, air, and water.

Selah receives two to three thousand kids a year, and at the end of their stay and their programs they stopped at the Country Store before going home. There David would deliver the Hes story. He then would ask, "How many of you kids, if you really wanted to, could physically touch and talk to a grandparent once a week?" David maintained that fewer than 25%, even of the local kids, have access to grandparents, since families are so spread out. He would say to the kids, "Those of you who raised your hands, you are the luckiest ones. Find out why your name is John or Maria. What kind of clothes did your mom wear when she was your age? What kind of toys did your dad play with? The best letter I got in my life came from a man who wrote, 'Dear Mr. Bamberger. I'm ninety-two years old. My granddaughter never gave a hoot about me until she came back from your place.' He said, 'Now, thank you, sir. She comes once a week with a clipboard and pencil asking me all kind of questions.' You've been studying nature and conservation while you were here, but you are the only people who can conserve your family history and your family heritage." It is certainly not hard to see why the Country Store and Hes' legacy elicit a deep, visceral response in the form of letters from parents and the kids themselves.

David was adamant about generating an interaction between parents and kids, as if he were vicariously making up for the levels of rejection he experienced in his own life. He astonished an audience of Girl Scouts and their leaders when a thirteen-year-old asked how she could help the environment. David responded, "Well, first I want to talk to you about emotion."

"What does that have to do with it?"

"Well, you may have to deal with some rejection from your neighbors. In order to overcome rejection, you have to arm yourself with knowledge so that you can defend your position." He advised the girl to discuss environmental issues with her parents and then ask them to promise not to fertilize the backyard or water the lawn or even cut the grass. A few months later, a Mr. Collins called David, saying his daughter was possessed and asking what would happen in his unkempt backyard. "Well, Mr. Collins, first let me congratulate you on participating in your daughter's concern for the environment. You will get something called 'plant succession' and that will provide a whole new world." Apparently, not the least examples of Mr. Collins's new world were one neighbor, irate over the appearance of rats and mice, and another, out of pity, offering to help with his spanking-new John Deere riding lawnmower.

David has also urged kids to rummage through the carport, check their closets and cupboards, and look under the kitchen and bathroom sinks, making a list of all the chemicals and compounds they discover in their homes. The vast quantity of products alone is almost always shocking and kids take particular glee in shaming their parents over their crimes against the natural world.

During my time in Johnson City, it became clear to me that exposing kids to nature had become a Selah priority. David would often go into a tirade over how much of American youth had been abandoned, and his solutions ranged from spinning back the clock to pre-feminism, believing mothers should provide fulltime care to their children, to advocating a socialistic, universal conscription to put youth, "the rich kid and the poor," to work for the nation, no one too good to do the most menial labor. His more conservative ideas shocked me at times, and even in his own family, where Donna was a fulltime homemaker providing for the children in the traditional sense, there were problems. But working in door-to-door sales for seventeen years and then for Church's Fried Chicken, which brought David to the most forsaken urban areas across America to buy real estate and set up management teams, gave him first-hand experience of American poverty and its violent consequences: gangs governing neighborhoods, soaring body counts, drugs, and alcohol abuse—all fueling a distinct culture for children. It was not out of naïveté but experience that David became committed to bringing inner city kids to Selah.

Selah had received a Still Water Grant to support an education project for inner-city middle school kids from Austin and San Antonio. The kids stayed at the ranch for several days to inspire their interest in the natural world and help them pass a required natural science examination. David was particularly keen on bringing what he called "lunch program children," inner-city kids who had no experience in an open nature preserve, and Colleen and Steven worked directly with Metz middle school in Austin.

While Selah programs targeted upper elementary and middle school kids, training teachers also became a focus. When dinosaur tracks were discovered on the ranch, Margaret acquired books, consulted experts, and visited museums to prepare a new teachers' workshop on Texas dinosaurs. She was working on her program during my first winter visit to Selah when we all stood on a rock ledge past Guzzler Loop and the fossil beds.

Mary and I could only think how unlikely it was to find dinosaur prints on top of a hill. David explained how Leroy had been capping the road and digging a runoff ditch when he found a deer that had been shot by the ledge. He called Randy to haul it out. Randy happened to look at the freshly uncovered rock and noticed a large, three-toed impression. He headed down to the ranch house and said off-handedly, "You know, if you really use your imagination, you might think there was a dinosaur footprint up on the hill." Margaret and David stopped dead whatever they were doing to follow Randy out to the ledge. As dirt was cleared off, more tracks were revealed on what had been a silty shore, the edge of a migrant ocean, where in one instant, eons ago, an *Acrocanthosaurus* passed, the moment imprinted in rock: squished muck, nail marks, the length of stride recorded now, hundreds of feet above sea level. While Leroy and the Mexicans built a small stone wall around the site and erected a sheet metal roof to slow erosion, Margaret assembled the educational program.

In so many ways, Margaret's coming to Selah was a life's dream come true for her, a place where her passions fit—studying nature, collecting plants, cataloging Selah's insects and mammals, joining bird counts, providing nature drawings, assembling manuals for workshops, and most importantly, leading groups and working with kids. Her interest in natural sciences, spurred by her work at the Highlands Nature Center, transformed into an obsession; she impulsively took courses in geology and natural sciences at Austin-area colleges, attended workshops, and fought for environmental causes.

David and Margaret had met in the mid-1990s, and after their inauspicious first dinner together David invited Margaret on a trip, first to Idaho and then up to Montana. Not long after, they showed up in Paris as lovers, on the pilgrimage to Bromfield's presbytery. Since then they've traveled extensively, including to Iceland, a geologists' paradise, with Mary and me, where I learned first-hand why David called Margaret such an ideal travel companion. While we crossed the heart of a volcanic wasteland, Margaret would breathe imaginative life into the desert and its creation of landmass, the very demarcation between Europe and America that none of us had

seen before. As much as David was comfortable at different social occasions, Margaret was plain seductive, a counterbalance of sensitivity and
earthiness next to David's brashness. Volunteers, birding groups, children,
and scientists alike adored her, having an easy comfort level with someone
on the same mission as David, but with a woman's touch.

The union took time to mature. Margaret's life was long established
in the Texas capital, where she had her family, the friends she loved, and
her work at the Austin Nature Center. David resided most of the time
in San Antonio, running his business operations. Ultimately they both
took the plunge, not only to move fulltime to Selah but also to have a
discrete wedding on the preserve.

Margaret poured herself into developing the education programs at
Selah, which grew from a larger concept. David had coined the expression
"people ranching," which Texas writer John Graves described in *National
Geographic:*

> David Bamberger . . . has studied the plight of native ranchers
> with concern and wants to do something about it. His prescrip-
> tion is what he calls "people ranching," which he practices along-
> side the standard sort. It consists essentially of providing rural
> experiences—along with healthy doses of land-stewardship train-
> ing—to urbanites shut off from such things in their daily lives.

Even Texas A&M University's department of recreation, park, and tourism sciences adopted, with David's permission, the expression "people
ranching" when describing the economic supplement of education and
nature tourism to ranching. David used the term specifically to mean
a healthy economic alternative to traditional, and more often than not,
unprofitable ranching. However, for a preserve dedicated to education,
habitat restoration, and the protection of endangered species, "people
ranching" took on a matrix of connotations, not the least of which is
manipulating people, as David would contend, toward what is dead
right. I would be the first to admit that I had been "people ranched"

myself at Selah. The future of Selah has become David's greatest pre-occupation, and he is well aware that in order to preserve his legacy and the ranch he has to generate public interest and recruit dedicated personnel, foundation members, and volunteers. Raising an endowment will require the people skills that have served David so well through his various professional manifestations. During my stay, I attended the Family Day Fundraiser with its country fair atmosphere and then the dedication of the greenhouse, half-built at the time and named for a generous donor to Selah.

I made friends with the front-line "people ranchers"—Scott, Steven, and Colleen—who have formed a Selah family and given youthful energy to Selah's programs. Steven and his wife Amanda had a baby, making the third generation of kids to spend their earliest years at the ranch, with Scott and Melissa Grote's kids Willow and Grey being the second. The first group of kids belonged Buddy, the cow Aggie, and Randy, the deer Aggie. They had two boys.

When David and Margaret realized they would have to focus their energies on building the foundation and securing the future of Selah as an independent preserve, they turned over the workshop and most of the administrative responsibilities to their new team. Frankly, the survival of Selah will depend in large part on engaging smart young environmentalists. Colleen Gardner has stepped into this role, taking over major responsibilities at the preserve.

Both David and Colleen love to recount their unlikely meeting in December 1999. David ritualistically sold Christmas trees with his fellow Optimist Club members for their annual fundraiser in Alamo Heights, outside San Antonio. David, seeing two women approach the lot, turned to his cohorts and boasted, "Just watch this now. I'm going to sell those beautiful women two Christmas trees." The women happened to be Colleen and her mother.

Colleen had just returned home from the Peace Corps in Niger, where she had been assigned to a maternity clinic administering care, family planning information, and oral vaccines for night blindness. The year she arrived, General Baré circumvented unfavorable election results with a *coup d'etat,* and ultimately the U.S., declaring the Niger government illegitimate, began pulling funds from USAID, crippling the clinic's efforts. Watching desperately needed supplies for the illiterate and impoverished women diminishing because of knee-jerk foreign policy decisions broke Colleen's heart. Two weeks back in the States and experiencing a kind of post-traumatic stress from culture shock if nothing else, she found herself waiting tables, talking often to overweight, boisterous people who had never heard of Niger, much less its dire plight. Growing embittered by dead-end conversations, she decided to keep her African experiences to herself and asked her mother to keep a lid on them, too.

David approached the women, asking what they were looking for. Colleen's mother responded that they wanted a special tree. They planned to celebrate their first Christmas in five years. This begged the question, "Why haven't you celebrated Christmas?"

Colleen, reluctant to tell her life story to a stranger, admitted, "Well, I've been out of the country." She didn't mention that her father died before she entered the Peace Corps, an experience so crushing that her family basically gave up on the holiday.

Colleen's mother walked to the tent to pay for the tree and on her return, David said, "You must be glad to have your daughter home for Christmas."

"You didn't tell him I was in Africa, did you?" Colleen asked looking crossly at her mother.

"No, I didn't tell him," Colleen's mother replied defensively.

"Where were you?" David asked.

"Niger in West Africa. No one has ever heard of it."

"I know Niger. I've been there twice." David explained the scimitar-horned oryx reintroduction program, and he and Colleen shared memories of the capital, Niamey, and recalled how dangerous the north had become with Khadafy-backed Taureg nomads controlling the region. They exchanged opinions on whether the flies were attracted to black or white and recalled sleeping on mats under the faultless stars.

"Where did you go to school?"

"Austin College. It's in Sherman. You probably don't know it."

"I've heard of Austin College. I'm on the advisory board. I help them with their environmental program." They shared intelligence on professors they knew in common.

"What are you doing now?"

"I have a business degree, but I'm pretty cynical about the corporate world. Right now I'm waiting tables at the Water Street Oyster Bar."

"I know Brad Lomax. I was a mentor to him."

Everything Colleen had done over the last decade came together in a string of fortuitous coincidences on a Christmas tree lot, and David invited Colleen and her mother to Selah for a full day. He delivered the complete, story-filled tour that ended with tears at Hes' Country Store. Margaret and David had already determined that they'd recruit Colleen as a volunteer. Colleen recalled, "I was blown away by what I perceived one person had done. I tried to remember everything David had shown and told in order to write about Selah to my Peace Corps friends. My mom thought coming to Selah might be a life changing moment for me, perhaps bigger than the Peace Corps. I was really scared that it would be just a glimpse, a passing experience."

Colleen immediately scheduled her days off at the restaurant to help out with Selah's school groups. A few months later, David and Margaret took a trip to Mexico to see the Monarch butterfly migration, and on returning they offered Colleen an unexpected internship. Overwhelmed with joy, she moved into a small corner apartment off the ranch house garage for eleven months and then moved into a hundred-year-old, one-room schoolhouse near Leroy's farm, where she experienced shades of the Peace Corps: no running water and a porous roof. For the first eleven months, David prepared a rigorous work regimen for Colleen. Her duties followed strict discipline in keeping with David's deeply held beliefs in hands-on knowledge, everything he still did himself, exposing her to all levels of Selah's operations including heavy physical labor—janitorial work, clearing brush, vaccinating calves, castrating goats, and hauling buckets of

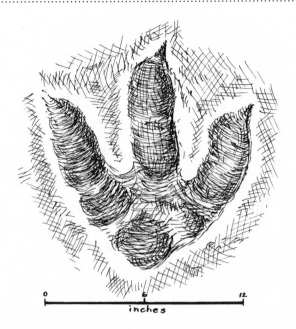

THERAPOD (MEAT EATER) DINOSAUR TRACK (FOOTPRINT)

water out of canyons to water saplings. It was an old-school apprenticeship. Multi-millionaire, executive director, or intern: no one is too important to clean toilets. Colleen attended every tour and workshop until she found herself giving talks on the oryx, benefited by her experience in Niger.

Even with all the training, Colleen was so terrified she could feel her cheeks shaking when she gave her first full tour of Selah while the Bambergers were off at a bat conference. A strong, dark-haired young man with a goatee attended that very tour, having received a flyer about Selah while working nearby for Texas Watch, then a part of the Texas Natural Resource Conservation Commission (now the Texas Commission on Environmental Quality). The young man turned out to be Scott Gardner, then a student in the geography department at what is now Texas State University in San Marcos. Scott fled inner-city Houston after high school for a small town in Montana, only to return three years later to manual labor. Fed up again with Houston, he enrolled in the university. He saw his future wife standing by the Blue Bonnet trailer, with a

PRAIRIE VERBENA *Glandularia bipinnatifida*

composure that never betrayed her inner panic. He was so besotted with her he'd gone practically deaf during her talk.

David predicted that Colleen would meet her mate at Selah, while Colleen remained skeptical. When I arrived at the ranch, stories and photographs of the wedding two years before still abounded. Some photographs featured Selah's black Amish carriage that transported the couple, David, and Colleen's mother to the ceremony. Colleen remembered, "When we were planning the wedding, my mom said to me that she wanted to share giving me away with David." David adored the occasion, giving away Colleen, his protégé, on the porch of Hes' Country Store on a clear, late October afternoon, all witnessed by two hundred guests.

The Relay for Life

THE BLANCO town center retains an authentic late nineteenth-century look with a broad oak-filled square dominated by a historic 1885 limestone courthouse. Featuring a square mansard roof, it is considered to be a good example of Second Empire architecture. The early stockmen, former Texas Rangers, and immigrants, who collectively displaced the less-than-delighted Comanches, would be dismayed to walk into any of their former buildings and see them now stocked with health foods, lavender products, postcards, woven earrings, and Harley Davidson fashion wear. However, some indigenous products have simply been improved: gourmet jerky and packaged wild flower seeds, for example.

Early in my stay in Johnson City, I thought I'd pick up a couple of cheap wineglasses at a second-hand store, but even in a part of Texas where wineries were replacing cattle ranches I was having little luck. I walked through rooms with antiques that might have found their way to Texas from just about anywhere, while a middle-aged woman, well acquainted with the shop owner, enjoyed a loud chat that betrayed no discernable Texas accent.

"I, for one, can not get excited about a man who races bicycles. I know everybody is mad about him. Look, he's just a man on a bicycle, for God's sake."

The shop owner offered no answer of her own as spring sunlight poured into her store, situated on the northeast corner of the square with large windows on two sides. Lance Armstrong, being an Austin resident who trains in the Hill Country, is understandably more than an international celebrity; he is a source of tremendous local pride for a sport that otherwise would hardly raise an eyebrow in a region sandwiched between football's Dallas Cowboys and basketball's San Antonio Spurs (let alone the pervasiveness of University of Texas and Texas A&M athletics and the state's two professional baseball teams). Living in France, I had only a passing interest in cycling, but I followed Lance Armstrong's victories year after year in the Tour de France, the most grueling endurance test of all major sports, and probably no less treacherous than boxing. He would ride the race-ending laps year after year in Paris, raising his glass of champagne to the chagrin of some, if not most, French sports writers who can't stomach an American setting records in their showcase event. Only a few months back in Paris after my stay in Johnson City, I walked from my apartment down to the shady crowd-lined Quai des Tuileries to watch the last victory laps of Lance's seventh and final Tour, a feat remarkable even for the "Bionic Man," much less a survivor of testicular cancer with metastases to the lung and brain. It was impossible not to get caught up in the personal story. Lance's lung capacity and muscle metabolism made him a thoroughbred for the sport, but more importantly he seemed to crave matching his iron will against excruciating pain.

When looking at Livestrong, The Lance Armstrong Foundation, one could compare some racing disciplines with cancer survivorship: "Unity is strength, knowledge is power, and attitude is everything." I had only vaguely heard of Livestrong and had no real knowledge of The Relay for Life, started in 1985 by Dr. Gordy Klatt, a colorectal surgeon, who put on an exceptional demonstration of his own endurance. For twenty-four hours, he ran and walked the stadium track at the University of Puget Sound. He covered over eighty-three miles while others came out to contribute small sums of money to the American Cancer Society for the privilege of briefly circling the track with him. The idea blossomed into hundreds of twenty-four hour relay events held nationwide to raise money for cancer research and patient support.

In the winter when I drove down to fog-bound Texas—trees, ponds, grasses, fences, and paved and unpaved roads absorbed in nightfall—I remember sitting with Margaret, and she turned to me and asked, "Have you ever dealt with a cancer patient?" The question cropped up out of nowhere and caught me off-guard. I think she was concerned I'd feel uncomfortable in her presence, but the answer was I'd never imagined that so many friends and family would have to face the dreadful ordeal of surgery, radiation, and chemotherapy, along with the emotional trauma. Still, I'd never known anyone who had made such an extraordinary comeback as Margaret, and I'd never thought carefully about the true nature of survival. At the time, Margaret was still weak; she wore support stockings to control swelling, and she had a filter implanted in her vena cava to prevent clots induced by the cancer from traveling to her lungs and brain. Nevertheless, she was filled with gratitude and liveliness.

David wore a yellow Livestrong gel bracelet, even though he certainly had little interest in cycling. In fact, he would readily launch into a rant against the waste of municipal resources and funding that go into building and maintaining professional sports complexes for events that only the middle class and the wealthy could afford while whole city neighborhoods remain without quality schools and employment opportunities. I walked with David when the cold clouds were descending on Selah, and we took the road behind Hes' Country Store up to the Recycle Cabin, which I hadn't seen. Hunters had rented it, but being friends they didn't mind David showing the place off. The building formed a clever conglomeration of time and place: the lighted fans came from the old Blue Bonnet Hotel in San Antonio, the windows were purchased for $15 from an old woman in D'Hanis, the counter was recovered from a failed TV repair shop, the front doors were selected from fifty David had collected, and the porch boards were salvaged from a cattle trailer. The cabin was set on the Mexicans' stonework. The planks mixed colors and wood tones; the simple lines and its setting in High Lonesome gave the building an original look and yet simultaneously a western atmosphere. David flashed with boyish enthusiasm and pride when describing the building that slept twelve and cost only $33,000 to build. However, the rest of the conversation centered on the late autumn, how poorly he'd dealt with Margaret's illness, and how dramatically unsettled the future had become. When critically ill, Margaret had asked for a Green Burial on the ranch, something David felt he should discuss with the family. He described a Green Burial, which had been growing increasingly popular. The idea struck me as both strange and beautiful, something akin to Hollywood westerns where pioneers would bury their dead in shallow makeshift graves where they would be most rapidly returned to the natural cycles of the land.

Four months later when I returned, David would remind me that Margaret was still a cancer patient, even though various tests revealed that her tumor, once diagnosed at stage four, had gone into total remission. She was one of the lucky patients for whom a controversial, molecularly targeted drug performed miracles. While she didn't present whole workshops, she began joining segments of tours to talk about Hill Country geology, Texas dinosaurs, the Chiroptorium, and the wildflowers. Some afternoons we'd pull nature books from shelves of the ranch house library and discuss the work of other illustrators. She showed me her drawings and details of the grasses, the oryx, the black-capped vireo, the golden-cheeked warbler, and the leaves and tree branches. She would still write David's correspondence and work on the herbarium, specimens collected, preserved, and catalogued for ranch records and future research.

While Selah's mission is sharing pure experiences in nature, creating a living classroom, the Bambergers often enough get caught in a pinch, finding themselves unexpectedly hosting a meal for fifty people. A scheduling error would produce a sudden apparition: an enthusiastic Audubon group expecting an inspirational tour and a hardy lunch. Colleen, swamped with her daily routine, would scramble over to The Center to prepare lasagna, salad, coffee, and cookies. Margaret would help host Selah board meetings, put together meals for visiting scientists staying at the Recycle Cabin, or attend organizational meetings that sometimes left her on the brink of exhaustion.

My time with David and Margaret made me consider the questions of survival and individual choices. Personal survival obviously overwhelms all other concerns. If one is able to attain basic physical needs, only then do social or psychological wants tend to become the personal focus. The innate tendency is to strive for greater respect, comfort, and acquisitions in a world that for the most part bases economic prosperity on production, merchandising, and entertainment, persuading us to buy what we don't need, systematically distracting us from the drudgery and rudimentary struggle for survival that the greater world population faces. It's hard to argue with such comfort, and it's impossible to argue against money equaling respect and power. So much of the brilliant environmental literature sounds the same alarm as Selah's historical marker; though almost playful in its appearance as the tombstone for mankind, its purpose is dead serious. The story of Selah is about moving people to take action, however quietly—even by simply respecting the ecosystems of their backyards, looking through their closets for dangerous, forgotten chemicals, and employing common sense about waste. Selah seeks to impart the notion that positive environmental action could become instinctive through exposure, understanding, and formation of good habits. Simply put, environmental protection makes personal sense.

David is fond of telling crowds, "It's my personal philosophy that nothing great is accomplished without enthusiasm." In a way, this statement echoes Armstrong's prescription for survival: "Attitude is everything." Moving people to action is tough business. Even Martin Luther King Jr. saw the complacency of friendly moderates as his biggest obstacle. How much loss of natural resources and plant and animal species is required? How many natural disasters will it take to move the individual heart to do so much as vote on behalf of the environment?

The future survival of Selah had been David's main preoccupation. He wanted to make a gift of the preserve to the National Audubon Society, The Nature Conservancy, and even to universities, but parks were struggling financially in the political climate of the U.S. Universities would construct dormitories and other buildings and overuse the fragile landscape he wanted to preserve. David wanted Selah to remain a natural classroom available to all economic classes without being spoiled by parking lots, signs, park fees, or even the commercialism of vending machines and a gift shop. David explained the problem to Karl Wolfshohl, writing for *Progressive Farmer:*

> State and national parks are in financial trouble and their infrastructure is crumbling, yet the population of America is going in droves to these places. Audubon tells me that the cost of operating a place like this runs 300 to 500% more than when a private landowner has it.

Wolfshohl very aptly characterized the difference:

> Why? Passion. Private landowners have a deep sense of pride in their ranches, working night and day to improve them without thought of payback. Not so for the average conservation-group or government employee.

David understands this intimately. It would be difficult to imagine the cost in salaries that just he and Margaret represent, not to mention how hard it would be to replace their know-how and experience. Once again, "attitude is everything." Peter Jennings and ABC got wind of Selah's plight and decided to run a feature on *World News Tonight.* The news producer called David to get directions from the San Antonio airport to the ranch. David said, "I'll meet you by the first cattle guard." The producer, imagining the "cattle guard" as a rather rough cowboy with a repeating rifle rather than galvanized steel bars on the road, responded, "Is it really that dangerous there?"

The television crew and trucks showed up and filmed the oryx, Madrone Lake, the Chiroptorium, and the Nature Trail for a three-minute segment to portray Selah's determination not to fall into the hands of developers. After the program, David received a call from the Johnson City postmaster. "Mr. Bamberger, you need to come down and pick up your mail." The mail turned out to be a mass outpouring of support for

Selah, bags of letters often containing a dollar, five dollars, ten. David was overwhelmed.

David told me that the National Audubon Society, somewhat embarrassed after the national news segment, offered to take Selah if David contributed two million dollars to support operating costs. David said, "Hell, I'll do it myself." He established Selah as a 501(c)3 organization and assembled a board of directors who believed in his philosophy. The board included his son and his faithful tree Aggie, Jim Rhoades. While I was at the ranch, David had spent days agitating before his first Selah board meeting. It was not only a matter of preparing a detailed report on the figures and future plans, but also on cleaning up the gallery at the ranch house. I helped him move display cases full of nests and dried seeds and transport furniture. He even experienced bizarre anxiety dreams: people from the past coming to the ranch house and refusing to leave. Margaret interpreted them as fear of losing control.

David was well aware of the difficulties Bromfield experienced in making Malabar Farm a public model of habitat restoration and an institution for environmental education. Bromfield had depleted his financial resources building up Malabar and starting or helping with similar models in Wichita Falls, Texas, and São Paulo, Brazil, bringing students from all over the world. Bromfield started a foundation called Friends of the Land, the legacy he hoped would carry on, but Doris Duke, tobacco heiress and friend of Bromfield's, had to step in and write a check to stave off loggers and save Malabar Farm while he was still alive. The Friends of the Land Foundation lasted only a year or two after Bromfield died. After sixteen years of debt and poor organization, Malabar was lifted out of limbo by the State of Ohio and the direction of Jim Berry, who arrived in 1972.

Berry said that one of the mistakes Bromfield made was failing to leave clear instructions for Malabar's future. David was keenly aware of two tasks that lay before him if Selah was to survive: to transform Selah into a recognized institution and to bestow an informing and inspirational vision. He had written a statement he called "My Vision for Selah," in which he discusses the future of the preserve. In it he expresses his fears of what might become of parks like Selah:

> What will parks and sanctuaries look like in the future? Will they glorify nature? Will they provide refuge for wild things, both animal and plant? Will the visitor be in the natural world, or one contrived or exploited with gift shops, restaurants, vending machines, vapor lights, cell phone towers, paved parking lots, sights, overused picnic areas, and garbage dumpsters? Will [the parks] be developed with buildings and machines, offices, computers, and large staffs? My vision, desire, and belief are the opposite. I truly believe that within twenty years there will be few, if any, publicly accessible parks or natural areas in America that will not have most or all of these things. There will be no places left except Selah that exclude all these signs of civilization, and with this "civilizing" of the natural world, Mother Nature suffers.

His dream is for purity, to perpetuate Selah through an inspired foundation, "a place that glorifies Mother Nature and shares it simply and cleanly with all others who visit."

During my spring in the Hill Country, I had a hard time keeping up with David and Margaret, who almost every evening attended lectures, dinner engagements, Selah celebrations for graduations and birthdays, big band dances, barbecues, festivals, and bat emergences. But the night that stood out most vividly was the Relay for Life survivor dinner at the First Baptist Church in Blanco, along with the testimonies, fundraising stalls, and the relay itself at Panther Stadium, ordinarily used for local school district football and track events. The church is a one-level brick building with an auditorium filled with the same tables David rented for the Family Day Fundraiser, except this time they were occupied by an astounding number of attendees clad in the purple t-shirts that cancer survivors were asked to wear. Margaret donned hers and was soon

absorbed with the organizers, support personnel, and other cancer survivors, while David registered us, made a donation, and then introduced
me to people he recognized.

We all sat down while Relay for Life volunteers, in this case high
school girls, served us pork loin, mashed potatoes, green beans, rolls, and
cake, along with soda or decaffeinated iced tea. A short inspirational
speech was followed by a formidable list of sponsors and organizers to
be thanked, along with a prayer from Brother Rusty Hicks, a man so
enormous he could have played as an offensive lineman in professional
football. A Baptist preacher, who, despite his spectacular size, blended
in perfectly with his rural community, his prayer was folksy, unadorned,
and affecting.

Four of those dining at our table wore purple t-shirts and all four had
suffered different forms of cancer with different procedures and results.
One had been playing football and broke his leg for no good reason;
another found a lump, wrongly diagnosed as benign, in her breast; and
a third had rectal cancer. Margaret and David had been on the way to
vacation with us in September in Sardinia when growing abdominal pain
waylaid Margaret in a Rome emergency room, where doctors, looking at
her abdominal ultrasound, advised her to go home as soon as possible.

Panther Stadium had a country-fair atmosphere by the time the
twenty-four hour Relay for Life was to begin, first with testimonials
and then a ceremonial lap by the survivors. The floodlights projected an
artificial whiteness over all of us, edged by Blanco's lights and distant
traffic on one side and on the other by the Blanco River flowing from the
west, the state park, and the Hill Country night with its spring aromas.
Margaret joined fellow survivors at the starting line while neighbors and
former employees came up to pay regards to David.

All around us stalls had been set up where families mingled, filling up
on fajitas, breakfast tacos, fried catfish, desserts, fruit cups, fruit drinks,
and ice cream. Some took pony rides, shot baskets, or tossed water bal-
loons, while the more adventurous in the crowd paid for wheelchair rides,
face painting, line dancing lessons, and massages. They even paid for

the privilege of playing jailhouse. Organizers had welcomed any clever idea that might bring in a dollar for the American Cancer Society while adding to the supportive, community atmosphere. The survivors started the relay, and David and I made the rounds of the stalls, most of which were erected just inside the sidelines of the football field, where the grass seemed surprisingly neglected in the off-season. We came to a mechanical roping game determined to give the operator fits. It had a statue-like horse; a kid with a lasso would be in the saddle, and a calf would present itself by moving out on a rail from between the horse's legs so it could be roped. Either the calf would remain frozen in place or shoot off down the rail before the child could blink, much less toss a rope. Inevitably, a little girl or boy would fling the lasso well after the calf was out of range. Only one Hispanic kid, almost expressionless, could manage to rope the rocketing calf. Scott showed up with Grey and Willow, and David went over to the operator and gave him a couple of dollar bills for the kids. Scott, an enthusiast of rodeo-level roping, coached the kids in leading the capricious calf, David shelling out more dollars, the operator fine-tuning the mechanism to no avail.

Seeing Grey and Willow at the Relay for Life made me think of how they were true Selah children, that their world of first memories begins with the Bamberger Ranch Preserve. David firmly believes in heritage. He adheres to the bucolic dream that one day a young Bamberger will come to Selah and feel deep pride in what his great-great grandfather accomplished for Mother Nature, thinking that being a Bamberger is indeed not at all a bad thing to be. As for his own children, David has deep regrets, sensing he lost them through his own force of personality, fretting about his dissipating powers of affluence, and the impotence common to so many parents when drug problems came up with their kids. But about restoring place, David delivered the altruistic understatement in an April 1997 interview for *The Economist:* "My whole objective is custodial: to leave the land in better condition than I found it."

Mourning for the environment appears to be another teardrop in an ocean of horrors. Why not own the "big house and Mercedes" that

David says we may have to do without? Preserving a world that we will not inhabit is in many ways a new exercise in the imagination, starting with those of us who inherited a world where mutually-assured destruction was the most feasible program politicians could devise to insure our survival. Maybe you have to be "a little goofy," as David would say, to think differently.

Central to the Relay for Life is the luminaria ceremony honoring the memory of those who have lost their battle with cancer. Friends and family received paper luminaria bags for making donations, and some chose to decorate them, adding the names of lost loved ones. The organizing committee and volunteers decorated the others, writing in donors along with the honored. They filled the bottoms of the bags with sand to hold them in place and added a candle. Once the purple t-shirted group had made its lap, others joined them, circling counterclockwise through the night and the next day. All along the outer edge, where it was dark, the illuminated paper sacks were spaced evenly with the candles lit inside them, the relay for life walkers and joggers passing them on a curving path. Survivorship has everything to do with the present.

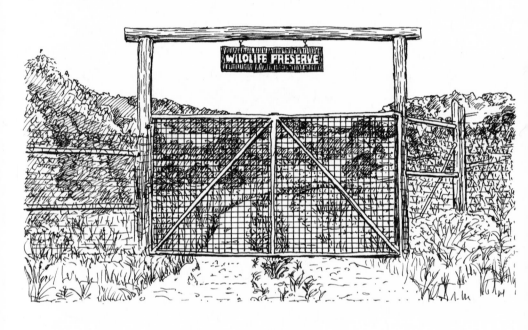

Works Cited

Anderson, Christopher. 9 December 2001. "Dispute Takes Wing over Area Bat Cave." *San Antonio Express-News:* 1A.

Bamberger, David. 1994. "Restoring Place: Demonstrating a Philosophy for the Future." *Heartland Voices* (Spring): 3–8.

Bamberger, David. 20 March 1995. *Endangered Species # 2.* Washington, D.C.: U.S. House of Representatives Committee on Resources.

Banks, Suzy. 8 March 1996. "A Call to the Wild: David Bamberger's Grand Obsession." *The Austin Chronicle:* 18, 22.

Belsie, Laurent. 2 September 1998. "Quest for a Cow that Thrives on Hot Sun and Brown Grass." *Christian Science Monitor.*

Bilger, Burkhard. 5 March 2001. "A Shot in the Ark." *The New Yorker:* 74–83.

"Blanco Exploiter Control Asked." 17 June 1977. *Blanco County News:* 10.

Bragg, Roy. 21 March 1995. "Federal Action Blasted at Species Act Hearing." *San Antonio Express-News:* 1A, 4A.

Bromfield, Louis. 1997. *Pleasant Valley.* Wooster: The Wooster Book Company.

Carson, Rachel. 1962. *Silent Spring.* London: Penguin Books.

Graves, John. April 1999. "Texas Hill Country." *National Geographic* 195:4: 105–20.

Hahn, Emily. 21 January 1991. "A Place and an Attitude." *The New Yorker:* 64–76.

Harrigan, Stephen. "The Balcones Escarpment." Read Me Texas. *Texas Monthly.* http://www.texasmonthly.com/ranch/readme/balcones.php/. Accessed 8 November 2005.

"How to be a green rancher." 12 April 1997. *The Economist*: 25.

Jennings, Diane. 17 December 1995. "Encouraging Herd." *The Dallas Morning News:* 45A, 48A–59A.

Kelley, Jo. Aug.–Sept., Oct.–Nov. 1992. "Interview with James Burnett." *Beefalo Nickel*. http://www.ababeefalo.org/ab120.htm.

McDonald, James R. 1995. "An Interview at Selah with David Bamberger." *Texas Studies Annual* 2: 165–79.

McKibben, Bill. 2003. *The End of Nature*. London: Bloomsbury.

Murphy, Michael A. May 2002. "Hill Country Heaven." *Texas Highways*: 34–41.

Sander, Susan M. Winter. 1997. "How to Build a Cave: A Bold Experiment in Artificial Habitat." *Bats* 15:4: 8–11.

Sugg, Ike C. 31 August 1992. "To Save an Endangered Species, Own One." *The Wall Street Journal*: A10.

Swanson, Eric R. 1995. *Geo-Texas: A Guide to the Earth Sciences*. College Station: Texas A&M University Press.

Texas Environmental Profiles. "5. Public Lands and Public Recreation." http://www.texasep.org/html/lnd/lnd_rpub.html. Accessed 13 November 2005.

Texas Property Tax Code. Title 1. Property Tax Code. Section 23.51. Definitions. http://www.window.state.tx.us/taxinfo/proptax/tc04/ch23d1.htm/. Accessed 14 February 2006.

Tuttle, Merlin D. 2003. *Texas Bats*. Austin: Bat Conservation International.

Wolfshohl, Karl. July 2001. "Who Wants Selah?" *Progressive Farmer*: 18.

Wordsworth, William. [1798]/1967. "Tintern Abbey." In *English Romantic Writers*. Ed. David Perkins.

Index

ISBN-13: 978-1-58544-593-6
ISBN-10: 1-58544-593-2